At Issue

How Can the Poor
Be Helped?

Other Books in the At Issue Series:

Age of Consent

Biodiversity

Can Busy Teens Succeed Academically?

Can Celebrities Change the World?

Club Drugs

Does the U.S. Two-Party System Still Work?

How Safe Is America's Infrastructure?

Nuclear Weapons

The Olympics

Polygamy

Teen Smoking

Teen Suicide

The U.S. Policy on Cuba

What Is the Future of the Music Industry?

What Is the Impact of E-Waste?

What Is the Impact of Tourism?

What Role Should the U.S. Play in the Middle East?

At Issue

How Can the Poor Be Helped?

Jennifer Dorman, Book Editor

GREENHAVEN PRESS
A part of Gale, Cengage Learning

Detroit • New York • San Francisco • New Haven, Conn • Waterville, Maine • London

GALE
CENGAGE Learning

Christine Nasso, *Publisher*
Elizabeth Des Chenes, *Managing Editor*

LIBRARY OF CONGRESS CATALOGING-IN-PUBLICATION DATA

How Can the Poor Be Helped? / Jennifer Dorman, book editor.
   p. cm. -- (At issue)
Includes bibliographical references and index.
ISBN 978-0-7377-5155-0 (hardcover) -- ISBN 978-0-7377-5156-7 (pbk.)
1. Public welfare--United States. 2. Public welfare. 3. Poverty. 4. Poor--Services for. I. Dorman, Jennifer. II. Title. III. Series.
HV91.H637 2011
362.5--dc22
                                                      2010050614

Printed in the United States of America
1 2 3 4 5   15 14 13 12 11

ED070

Contents

Introduction   7

1. Welfare Reforms Have Been Successful   12
   in Helping America's Poor
   Jeff Jacoby

2. Welfare Reforms Have Not Been   16
   a Complete Success
   Katha Pollitt

3. Government Programs Should Be More   21
   Tailored to America's Poor
   Margaret Simms

4. Government Welfare Hurts Society   26
   and Does Not Benefit the Poor
   The Libertarian Party

5. Education Can Help People out   30
   of Poverty
   Michelle Rhee

6. Is Education the Cure for Poverty?   35
   Jared Bernstein

7. Marriage Reduces Poverty   42
   Robert Rector

8. Marriage Is Not the Answer to Poverty   50
   Polly Toynbee

9. Raising the Minimum Wage Will Help   55
   the Poor
   Holly Sklar

10. Wage Regulation Will Not Help the Poor   66
    Bill Barnes

11. Capitalism Is the Cure for Poverty   73
    Robert Gelinas

12. Unregulated Capitalism Exploits the Poor   78
    Barbara Ehrenreich

13. Africa Needs Trade More than Aid   82
    William Easterly

14. Microfinance Can Alleviate Poverty   87
    Daniel Howden

Organizations to Contact   92

Bibliography   97

Index   101

Introduction

In 2000, world leaders came together at the United Nations Headquarters and pledged their commitment to significantly reduce global poverty by 2015. The targets they outlined, known as the Millennium Development Goals (MDGs), generated a concerted effort to find better ways to fight poverty. Since then, one policy that has proliferated rapidly is conditional cash transfers (CCTs). CCTs provide money for families in need, usually on a monthly basis, to help meet specific requirements such as medical exams or funds that facilitate children to attend school. Data on these programs is abundant and indicates that they have a considerable positive impact on both poverty and behavior. While there are concerns, including the limits of this model as well as the use of conditions, CCTs now exist in developing countries throughout the world and were even the subject of a recent experiment in New York City.

CCTs are considered an alternative to traditonal welfare, and offer a way for governments to do two things at once. According to Tim Ogden and Anders Gustafson, CCTs link governments and individuals in a mutually beneficial social contract—extremely poor families receive cash assistance and "for the government, the program's conditions help promote long-term investments in human capital which will hopefully lower the cost of future social services."[1] Human capital is measured in terms of health, education and other outcomes that don't provide an immediate financial return. In developinng countries, it is common for children to forgo school in order to provide care for younger siblings so their parents can work, or for the children to go to work themselves. In many of these countries, education is not viewed as an investment in the fu-

---

1. Tim Ogden and Anders Gustafson, "Paying Parents to Keep Kids in School," *Philanthropy Action*, April 23, 2008.

ture but instead as a squandering of current resources. By making government assistance contingent on these kind of investments, CCT programs hope to break the cycle of generational poverty, where successive generations of a family find themselves in the same, dire financial situation as their parents and grandparents, with no prospect of overcoming the difficulty.

Because the CCT concept is so basic, programs comes in many shapes and sizes. Two of the oldest and most popular programs are Oportunidades in Mexico and Bolsa Familia in Brazil, covering nearly 5 million and 12 million families respectively. These programs, started in the 1990s, have been studied extensively and replicated in several other countries. Today, CCTs exist in at least 40 countries, including Ecuador, Chile, Jamaica, Bolivia, Malawi, Turkey, and the Philippines. Programs differ from place to place, and include a wide selection of services such as regular medical checkups, pre- and post-natal visits, vaccines, school attendance, and parenting classes. Programs also vary in the amount of cash they offer and the timing of the transfers. As these programs continue to evolve, several studies are underway to test the different variables for maximum effectiveness. In an article about CCTs for the Center for Strategic and International Studies, Jennifer Lerner writes that "the provision of much-needed supplemental income for the poor, the decrease in income inequality, and incentives to keep children in school and healthy, are certainly important and crucial steps in the right direction," and that "despite their flaws, CCTs are working to tackle poverty in creative and effective ways."[2]

Though positive outcomes with CCTs are well-documented, it is not completely clear whether conditionality is the key to their success. For many critics, CCTs represent an untenable paternalism because they essentially imply that

2. Jennifer Lerner, "Conditional Cash Transfers in Latin America: An Examination of Oportunidades and Bolsa Familia," Center for Strategic and International Studies, August 3, 2010.

poor people are not capable of knowing what's best for them. According to Steven Devereux of the Institute of Development Studies, data on unconditional cash transfers (UCTs) from several African countries show that recipients invest some of their cash transfers in education and health anyway, "so there is no need to compel them to do so."[3] However, a report published via the World Bank, "Conditional Cash Transfers: Reducing Current and Future Poverty," by Ariel Fiszbein and Norbert Schady, defends the need for paternalism in cases where individuals "hold persistently erroneous beliefs," are dealing with conflicts in the household, or are not motivated to act with long term vision. Conditionality also adds layer of buy-in from people who would not otherwise want their money used for welfare "handhouts," note Fiszbein and Schady.[4] Therefore CCTs can appeal to a larger swath of the political spectrum.

CCTs are indeed such a politically popular initiative that many are concerned that governments will see them as a panacea. However, the high usage of services does not guarantee the quality of the services being utilized. For example, Hugo Florez, of the Inter-American Development Bank, warns that "CCTs don't solve the problem of quality of education, and they don't improve the kinds of health services that are available, either."[5] Some believe that increasing the demand for services will lead to their improvement, but currently there is little evidence to support this idea. Additionally the Fiszbein/ Schady report points out that "even the best-designed CCT program cannot meet all the needs of a social protection system. It is, after all, only one branch of a larger tree that includes workfare, employment, and social pension programs."

3. Steven Devereux, "Cash Transfers: to Condition or Not to Condition," *Eldis* of the Institute of Development Studies, 2009.
4. Ariel Fiszbein and Norbert Schady, "Conditional Cash Transfers: Reducing Current and Future Poverty," The World Bank, 2009.
5. Inter American Development Bank, "The End of Inherited Poverty," September 2, 2009.

Until recently, CCT programs were employed solely by developing countries. However, in 2007, New York City launched a three-year, privately-funded CCT experiment modeled after Mexico's Oportunidades. Named Opportunity NYC, the New York City program offered a stipend to a select group of participants to meet conditions such as dental visits, employment, and school attendance by their children. While many saw great potential in the initiative and positive early outcomes, Mayor Michael Bloomberg was ultimately not impressed enough to make it into a public program and ended the experiment after three years. Megan Cottrell of the blog *True/Slant*, disagreed with Bloomberg's decision, writing that the "New York CCT program helped families make ends meet." She also noted that participants in the program were more likely to have a bank account versus non-participants, indicating a positive lifestyle outcome that could continue into the future.[6]

As reported by the *New York Times*, Mayor Bloomberg admitted that some aspects worked while others didn't. Announcing his decision to discontinue the program, Bloomberg added his voice to a universal lament:

> "You always hope that you'll come across a magic silver bullet, and you never do," he said. "If there were simple solutions, somebody would have found them a long time ago. And you make progress incrementally, particularly if you're trying to focus on some of society's biggest problems."[7]

CCTs will continue to be a major tool in the anti-poverty arsenal, specializing and evolving into more successful programs that may help people out of poverty whether they live in the most underdeveloped rural village or an urban center of the developed world. But ideas on how to alleviate poverty in

6. Megan Cottrell, "Paying the Poor to Do Right Doesn't Work. Or Does It?" *True/Slant*, April 12, 2010.
7. Floyd Whaley, "A Different Kind of Aid: Hand Out Money," *New York Times*, March 5, 2010.

general are extremely varied. The viewpoints expressed in *How Can the Poor Be Helped?* cover a range of opinions on how to deal with one of the world's greatest challenges.

1

Welfare Reforms Have Been Successful in Helping America's Poor

Jeff Jacoby

Jeff Jacoby is a journalist and recipient of the Breindel Prize for excellence in opinion journalism and the Thomas Paine Award of the Institute for Justice. He has been an op-ed columnist for the Boston Globe *since 1994.*

In 1996, Bill Clinton signed welfare reform into law amid warnings of doom from opponents, including members of his own Democratic party. Ten years later, welfare reform holds up as one of Clinton's most successful achievements. The law resulted in a drastic drop in the number of people on welfare and a corresponding rise in employment among those formerly dependent on the state. Far from causing children to starve, as critics had warned, poverty among children declined significantly as well.

Lillie Harden was a 32-year-old mother of three from Little Rock, Ark., when Bill Clinton met her at a panel on reforming welfare in 1986. Harden had collected welfare for two years before finding work and had come to speak about her experience. Clinton asked her what was best about being off welfare. Her reply: "When my boy goes to school and they say, 'What does your mama do for a living?' he can give an answer."

Ten years later, when Clinton was in the White House, he invited Harden to join him as he signed the Personal Respon-

sibility and Work Opportunity Reconciliation Act of 1996—
welfare reform—into law. In his remarks, Clinton recalled her
answer of a decade earlier, and added: "I have never forgotten
that."

For all that Clinton got wrong, welfare reform was one
thing he ended up getting very right. He had vetoed two previous reform bills passed by the Republican-controlled Congress, and when the House and Senate came back with a third
bill, liberal pressure for another veto was intense. But political
strategist Dick Morris warned Clinton that a third veto could
cost him the 1996 election, and so, pronouncing it a "historic
opportunity to do what is right," he signed the bill.

Criticism from the Left

The chorus of outrage from the left was deafening. Marian
Wright Edelman, chairman of the Children's Defense Fund,
warned that Clinton's signature would "leave a moral blot on
his presidency and on our nation." Senator Patrick Leahy of
Vermont denounced the bill as "anti-family, anti child, and
mean-spirited." Hugh Price, head of the National Urban
League, declared that "Washington has decided to end the War
on Poverty and begin a war on children." Over and over it was
said that welfare reform would wreak social devastation,
throwing vast numbers of people, including a million children, into poverty.

---

*For the first time, Welfare would come with strings at-
tached: work requirements and time limits designed to
encourage responsibility and self-sufficiency.*

Peter Edelman, the husband of Marian Wright Edelman
and an assistant secretary of health and human services, re-
signed in protest and condemned the new law in a long article—"The Worst Thing Bill Clinton Has Done"—in *The Atlantic*. It predicted, among other things, "more malnutrition

and more crime, increased infant mortality, and increased drug and alcohol abuse . . . increased family violence and abuse against children and women." He concluded, this "terrible legislation" would do "serious injury to American children."

It did none of those things.

Ten Years of Success

What it *did* do was end the condescending attitude that the poor were incapable of improving their situation, and that "compassion" consisted of supplying money indefinitely to women who had children, but no husbands or jobs. That approach had lured millions into lives of dependency, subsidized an explosion of fatherlessness, and infected neighborhoods with a bias against work and marriage. The bill that Clinton signed replaced deadly condescension with respect. For the first time, welfare would come with strings attached: work requirements and time limits designed to encourage responsibility and self-sufficiency.

The results speak for themselves. Since peaking in 1994, the nation's welfare caseload plummeted by 60 percent, falling from 5 million families to fewer than 2 million. Welfare recipients went to work in droves. The employment rate among those who had been likeliest to slip into long-term dependence—young mothers who had never been married—soared by nearly 100 percent. And as more and more mothers left welfare and got jobs, more and more of their children were lifted out of poverty.

Far from throwing a million kids into the streets, welfare reform sent the child poverty rate tumbling, from 20.8 percent in 1995 to 17.8 percent in 2004. In black communities, where welfare had done the most damage, the decline was even more dramatic. "Black child poverty plummeted at an unprecedented rate, falling to 30.0 percent in 2001," Robert Rector of the Heritage Foundation testified before Congress. "In 2001, despite the recession, the poverty rate for black children was at the lowest point in national history."

Reform Is Still Needed

Not everything has been reformed. The 1996 law affected only the basic welfare program, Aid to Families with Dependent Children. But dozens of other welfare entitlements, such as food stamps and Medicaid, still operate under the old rules. And while the out-of-wedlock birth rate is no longer skyrocketing, it is still far too high—as are the poverty and social chaos it begets.

That said, it is clear that welfare reform has been a shining success. The Republican Congress that passed it and the Democratic president who signed it turned out to be truer champions of the poor than those who inveighed against it so hysterically.

2

Welfare Reforms Have Not Been a Complete Success

Katha Pollit

Katha Pollitt is a poet and essayist. She writes the "Subject to Debate" column for The Nation.

Plummeting welfare rolls and rising employment rates, often touted as the indicators that prove the effectiveness of welfare reform, do not tell the whole story. In many cases, employment for single mothers meant low wage jobs that hardly lifted their families out of poverty. With current employment rates for middle-class families at historically low levels, the fate of those who were living below the poverty line before welfare reform was enacted is even more imperiled. The fact that relatively fewer people are turning to welfare now suggests that the reformed policy is not reaching those who need it.

Long lines of gloomy people in business suits at a jobs fair. Foreclosure signs on tidy suburban lawns. Adults moving into their parents' basement. In the news these days, the face of poverty is middle class, educated and often married: the hard-working, play-by-the-rules victims of the ongoing financial crisis. It's the man-bites-dog story that never ends.

But what about the people who already were poor before the crisis? Like women on welfare? Oh, them. The welfare reform bill, pompously titled the Personal Responsibility and Work Opportunity Reconciliation Act of 1996 (PRWORA) and signed by Bill Clinton in the run-up to the election, was supposed to pull these hapless folk off the dole with a mix of carrots and sticks aimed at forcing mothers off welfare and into the workforce. Not only would they find jobs that would allow them to support their children, the theory went; once single motherhood ceased to be subsidized by the taxpayer, poor women would settle down and marry before having kids. On its tenth anniversary PRWORA was widely trumpeted as a success: "Pragmatic progress," declared *Newsweek*'s Robert Samuelson. "Everything has worked," Douglas Besharov of the American Enterprise Institute told *USA Today*. "Welfare reform has been a triumph for the federal government and the states—and even more for single mothers," claimed Brookings Institution senior fellow Ron Haskins in its newsletter. On the *New York Times* op-ed page, Clinton patted himself on the back for a successful triangulation ("At the time, I was widely criticized by liberals who thought the work requirements too harsh and conservatives who thought the work incentives too generous") and for moving millions from "dependence to empowerment."

Low Wage Employment

True, the widespread disaster—1.1 million newly poor children, for instance—predicted by some opponents did not come about: child poverty actually went down. Millions of welfare mothers found work, albeit often casual, low-wage jobs that did not lift them out of poverty. How much of a triumph is it that in the late 1990s, 65 percent of former recipients in South Carolina were working, earning an average hourly wage of $6? Or that in Maryland, in one quarter, about half of former recipients had found work at pay that annualized to roughly $9,500—way below the poverty line for an average family? In a New York City study I wrote about in February 1999, only 126 former recipients out of a sample of 569 even had valid phone numbers, hardly a sign of prosperity and stability; of the 126, 58 percent were supporting their families "mainly through work," and the median wage was $7.50.

Welfare Reform and Single Motherhood

But those women were entering the workforce at a moment of labor-force expansion and prosperity in the US economy; 16 million jobs were created in the 1990s. And even then—with a good jobs market, well-funded transitional programs and federal and state coffers flush with tax dollars—most welfare mothers stayed poor. Some, indeed, became poorer than ever, a development that tended to be briefly noted, if at all. As for the effects PRWORA was supposed to have on sexual mores, teen pregnancy did go down—but that happened for many reasons, and the United States is still way out in front of the other industrialized nations, including those with generous supports for young mothers and their children. Single motherhood continued to rise, accounting for 41 percent of all births in 2008, a historic high. Since single motherhood is rising all over the world, in countries from Ireland to Japan, it is not surprising that it has proved resistant to PRWORA's supposed miracle cure.

No one sane assumes that today's unemployed are loafing, that jobs are "out there" for them or that getting married would solve their problems.

The Economic Downturn Creates a New Poor

If the boom years failed to lift poor mothers into the middle class, how are they faring now that the middle class is becoming the new poor? The fact that the welfare rolls have risen less than 10 percent since December 2007 while food stamp use has soared by 40 percent—an amazing one in eight Americans now uses them—suggests that welfare isn't reaching poor families: either women who apply are being turned away, or the programs are so minimal, or so onerous, that people aren't signing up. How do they manage? Sharon Hays, author of *Flat Broke With Children: Women in the Age of Welfare Reform*, writes in an e-mail, "They get by in the same way the poor of New Orleans and Haiti are getting by, by cobbling together every available source of aid and support, and then trying to learn how to adjust to constant suffering and insecurity. Increasing rates of domestic violence are just one hidden story here." And what about women who have reached their state's time limit—two years, three years, five years—and can't get welfare *for the rest of their lives*? Jane Collins, the author, with Victoria Mayer, of *Both Hands Tied: Welfare Reform and the Race to the Bottom of the Low-Wage Labor Market*, writes, "In Wisconsin, most people who have used up their time limits are simply out of luck."

Sounds like the laid-off workers for whom Congress recently capped unemployment benefits at ninety-nine weeks— but their situation, unlike that of welfare mothers, evokes widespread sympathy No one sane assumes that today's unemployed are loafing, that jobs are "out there" for them or that getting married would solve their problems. If you think about it, though, given that PRWORA has been in effect for nearly fifteen years, it would not be difficult for a mother to reach the lifetime limit, even in Wisconsin, where it's a comparatively generous sixty months.

Empowering Women in Poverty

I asked Collins if she saw anything good in welfare reform. "It was always a stigmatized program, a football in racial politics. If it were possible to make unemployment and other entitlement programs gender sensitive—to take account of caregiving, for example, and the need for childcare—and put women into these mainstream programs instead of welfare, that would reconceive poor mothers as economic citizens, as workers with rights. And that would be good." But for that to happen, people would have to care.

3

Government Programs Should Be More Tailored to America's Poor

Margaret Simms

Margaret Simms is a Senior Fellow at the Urban Institute in Washington, D.C. Prior to joining the Urban Institute, she was a vice president at the Joint Center for Political and Economic Studies.

Current approaches to poverty reduction promote employment for all who can work without understanding the varying needs that exist within poor populations. Immigrant groups require more language training; single mothers do not receive adequate child care, and African Americans often face physical barriers to centers of economic opportunity. No matter how motivated people are to work, without targeted supports, they will not be able to escape poverty.

> *The time has come for us to civilize ourselves by the total, direct and immediate abolition of poverty.*
>
> —*Martin Luther King, Jr.,*
> *"Where Do We Go from Here: Chaos or Community?" 1967*

It has been said that we are entering a new era of government policy. If so, it could be an opportune time to belatedly heed the call of Dr. Martin Luther King and revamp our policies toward the poor. Over the past decade we have moved

Margaret Simms, "Tailoring Assistance: How Antipoverty Policy can Address Diverse Needs Within the Poverty Population," *Spotlight on Poverty*, N.D. Reproduced by permission.

from a set of policies that provided cash assistance (mostly inadequate) to people who were in need (by standards set by the government) to one in which those who can work are expected to do so. In the process, we have ignored the fact that the poor are not a homogeneous group of people, all of whom can and will work if they have no other means of support. They are, in fact, quite diverse. Recognizing this diversity is a necessary prerequisite for developing effective antipoverty policies.

Poverty Statistics

According to the U.S. Census Bureau, 12.5 percent of the U.S. population (over 37 million) was below the poverty line in 2007. While non-Hispanic whites are the largest group in poverty (16 million, or 43 percent of the total), the poverty population is disproportionately minority. Over one-quarter are African American and a similar percentage are Hispanics of all races. Children constitute a third of the poverty population, many of them living in single-mother families. If we do not address the needs of these children, we don't just fail to reduce the current poverty population, we multiply our future problems. Poor children often lack access to the services and opportunities needed to move up the economic ladder when they reach adulthood unless the public sector provides that access.

The breakdown of children in poverty shows them almost equally divided by race and ethnicity, with each major group (non-Hispanic whites, African Americans, and Hispanics) constituting about one-third of the total. But the chances of being poor are higher if you are an African American or Hispanic child than if you are an Asian or non-Hispanic white child.

The chance of being poor is also higher if the child is in a female-headed family. Fifty-nine percent of poor children are in female-headed families, and the poverty rate for children in

these families is 43 percent. Put these two factors together—
being an African American or Hispanic child living in a
female-headed family and you have a one in two chance of
being poor, compared with a one in three chance if you are a
white child in a female-headed family.

---

*As we think about how to expand employment opportu-
nities for these individuals, we should keep their special
circumstances in mind.*

Approximately 22 percent of all children in the United
States under the age of 18 are the children of immigrants. The
poverty rate among these children (slightly more than one-
half of whom are Hispanic) is nearly 40 percent higher than it
is among children of the native born. One-half of these children are in low-income families, despite the fact that their
parents have relatively high work effort.

Clearly any strategy for reducing poverty in the long run
must reach children. But doing so often involves helping their
parents or other adults in the households in which they live.
Over the past decade, our principal strategy for doing this has
been through promoting work effort. Knowing more about
the characteristics of these families helps us assess what strategies are likely to be effective in helping them escape poverty.

At the present time, finding and keeping a job is a challenge for many workers. But it may be especially true for
those in poor or low-income (below 200 percent of the poverty line) families. As we think about how to expand employment opportunities for these individuals, we should keep their
special circumstances in mind.

Understanding Disparities Creates Better Strategies

African American and Hispanic families are more likely to be
unemployed and to work at low wages. A forthcoming paper

by Urban Institute researchers Gregory Acs and Pamela Lo-prest ("Working for Cents on the Dollar: Race and Ethnic Wage Gaps in the Noncollege Labor Market") indicates that low-wage work opportunities are different for the two groups, suggesting that different policies or strategies are needed to improve their economic conditions. While both African Americans and Hispanics are likely to have low levels of education compared with their white counterparts, educational differences explain more of the wage disparities between non-Hispanic whites and Hispanics than they do the wage disparities between non-Hispanic whites and African Americans.

Regardless of race and ethnicity, single mothers have a difficult time balancing work and family.

For Hispanics, policies might be oriented toward improving their educational and skill levels and, for immigrants, also improving English language skills. While more education and training will help African Americans, they are likely to need additional policies to help them advance. Some of the difficulties African Americans face may be due to their relative isolation from places of economic opportunity. Any policies to promote employment will need to take this fact into account by also expanding the supply of affordable housing in opportunity-rich neighborhoods, increasing job opportunities in communities in which African Americans live, improving transportation, or some combination of these policies.

The Challenges of Single Motherhood

Regardless of race or ethnicity, single mothers have a difficult time balancing work and family. Work supports that boost their income and provide access to child care are important for women who head families without a partner present. But low-wage workplaces rarely provide the types of supports that parents need in order to help their children develop through parental participation in school activities and consultation with their children's teachers. Moreover, the children lack access to quality child care and early education programs that would facilitate cognitive development and socialization. As part of an Urban Institute initiative to develop a New Safety Net, researchers Shelley Waters Boots, Jennifer Macomber, and Anna Danziger outline a set of policies that would support parents' employment and also facilitate children's development. These include flexible work schedules, paid leave, and comprehensive family supports through greater funding for Early Head Start, increased child care subsidies, and stronger connections between the child care subsidy system and work supports.

Sustained Employment Requires Targeted Supports

If we are going to make a serious dent in poverty, the United States will have to develop an integrated set of policies that address the diverse and interrelated needs of the poor and, more broadly, the low-income population. Promoting employment without addressing issues of skills training, discrimination, and physical isolation will not lift low-income working families out of poverty and into the middle class. Putting mothers in the labor force without addressing their children's needs will only roll the problems forward to the next generation.

Some might argue that we cannot address these issues during tough economic times, but tough times often provoke bold solutions. Let us hope this is one of those times.

4

Government Welfare Hurts Society and Does Not Benefit the Poor

The Libertarian Party

The Libertarian Party is America's third-largest political party. It encourages limited government and supports the rights of the individual.

The welfare system, which is unfair to taxpayers and doesn't help the poor lift themselves out of poverty, should be abolished. Those who require help should turn to resources outside of the government. In order to address poverty, barriers to business ownership must be mitigated and primary education options need to be improved. Temporary assistance for those who fall on hard times should come from private charities.

From across the political and ideological spectrum, there is now almost universal acknowledgement that the American social welfare system has been a failure.

Since the start of the "war on poverty" in 1965, the United States has spent more than $5 trillion trying to ease the plight of the poor. What we have received for this massive investment is—primarily—more poverty.

Our welfare system is unfair to everyone: to taxpayers who must pick up the bill for failed programs; to society, whose mediating institutions of community, church and family are increasingly pushed aside; and most of all to the poor them-

The Libertarian Party, "Poverty and Welfare," May 9, 2008. Reproduced by permission.

selves, who are trapped in a system that destroys opportunity for themselves and hope for their children.

The Libertarian Party believes it is time for a new approach to fighting poverty. It is a program based on opportunity, work, and individual responsibility.

End Welfare

None of the proposals currently being advanced by either conservatives or liberals is likely to fix the fundamental problems with our welfare system. Current proposals for welfare reform, including block grants, job training, and "workfare" represent mere tinkering with a failed system.

It is time to recognize that welfare cannot be reformed: it should be ended.

We should eliminate the entire social welfare system. This includes eliminating AFDC [Aid to Families with Dependent Children], food stamps, subsidized housing, and all the rest. Individuals who are unable to fully support themselves and their families through the job market must, once again, learn to rely on supportive family, church, community, or private charity to bridge the gap.

If the federal government's attempt at charity has been a dismal failure, private efforts have been much more successful. America is the most generous nation on earth. We already contribute more than $125 billion annually to charity. However, as we phase out inefficient government welfare, private charities must be able to step up and fill the void.

To help facilitate this transfer of responsibility from government welfare to private charity, the federal government should offer a dollar-for-dollar tax credit for contributions to private charities that provide social-welfare services. That is to say, if an individual gives a dollar to charity, he should be able to reduce his tax liability by a dollar.

Tear Down Barriers to Economic Growth

Almost everyone agrees that a job is better than any welfare program. Yet for years this country has pursued tax and regulatory policies that seem perversely designed to discourage economic growth and reduce entrepreneurial opportunities. Someone starting a business today needs a battery of lawyers just to comply with the myriad of government regulations from a virtual alphabet soup of government agencies: OSHA [Occupational Safety and Health Administration], EPA [Environmental Protection Agency], FTC [Federal Trade Commission], CPSC [Consumer Product Safety Commission], etc. Zoning and occupational licensing laws are particularly damaging to the type of small businesses that may help people work their way out of poverty.

We call for the repeal of government regulations and taxes that are steadily cutting the bottom rungs off the economic ladder.

In addition, government regulations such as minimum wage laws and mandated benefits drive up the cost of employing additional workers. We call for the repeal of government regulations and taxes that are steadily cutting the bottom rungs off the economic ladder.

Reform Education

There can be no serious attempt to solve the problem of poverty in America without addressing our failed government-run school system. Nearly forty years after Brown vs. Board of Education, America's schools are becoming increasingly segregated, not on the basis of race, but on income. Wealthy and middle class parents are able to send their children to private schools, or at least move to a district with better public schools. Poor families are trapped—forced to send their children to a public school system that fails to educate.

It is time to break up the public education monopoly and give all parents the right to decide what school their children will attend. It is essential to restore choice and the discipline of the marketplace to education. Only a free market in education will provide the improvement in education necessary to enable millions of Americans to escape poverty.

Hard Times Require Compassion and Charity

We should not pretend that reforming our welfare system will be easy or painless. In particular it will be difficult for those people who currently use welfare the way it was intended—as a temporary support mechanism during hard times. However, these people remain on welfare for short periods of time. A compassionate society will find other ways to help people who need temporary assistance. But our current government-run welfare system is costly to taxpayers and cruel to the children born into a cycle of welfare dependency and hopelessness.

The Libertarian Party offers a positive alternative to the failed welfare state. We offer a vision of a society based on work, individual responsibility, and private charity. It is a society based on opportunity and genuine compassion it is a society built on liberty.

5

Education Can Help People out of Poverty

Michelle Rhee

Michelle Rhee is the former Chancellor of the District of Columbia Public Schools.

By building on models of success, society can dramatically improve public education and turn the tide of generational poverty. Allocating resources and following proven methods of success will require long term vision and commitment on the part of politicians and educators. Education must become a priority to give children the tools they need to overcome poverty.

"I remember in elementary school—did you guys do this?—switching clothes every other morning with my best friends. That way nobody could tell we each only had one pair of jeans and a t-shirt." Heads nodded in recognition at this meeting of [Washington] DC public school seniors reflecting on their early years.

Students in our public schools are my best sources on what it is like to strive in a school system that has not given them an equal shot in life. With 70 percent of them receiving a free or reduced-price lunch and with DC's child poverty rate well above the national average, poverty is a mountain that children in our nation's capital climb daily.

This particular group of students had beaten the odds, and they were advancing to college. But they worried that

Michelle Rhee, "Ending Poverty Through Education," *Spotlight on Poverty*, Februrary 8, 2010. Reproduced by permission.

they were unprepared. With only 9 percent of our entering high school freshmen graduating from college within 5 years of high school, and an unemployment rate that has more than doubled with the recession, they were right to be concerned.

Improving Education Requires Resolve

I believe we can solve the problems of urban education in our lifetimes and actualize education's power to reverse generational poverty. But I am learning that it is a radical concept to even suggest this. [American investor] Warren Buffett framed the problem for me once in a way that clarified how basic our most stubborn obstacles are. He said it would be easy to solve today's problems in urban education.

"Make private schools illegal," he said, "and assign every child to a public school by random lottery." Think about what this would mean. CEOs' children, diplomats' children, many would be going to schools in Anacostia and east of the river, where most of our schools are. I guarantee we would never see a faster moving of resources from one end of the city to the other. I also guarantee we would soon have a system of high-quality schools.

As the leader of a school system in a privileged country, I know we cannot have the same conversation about poverty in developing nations as we can about urban and rural poverty in the United States. But when we ask what it will take to ensure that no child anywhere has to "beat the odds" to have viable future choices, the answer is the same whether we are in Washington, DC or in a brave Haiti enduring disaster from a poverty-stricken stance. The obstacle is not one of knowledge but of social and political will, with education as the lynchpin.

Finding Examples of Success

On global poverty, economist and author Jeffrey Sachs created a splash with his argument that we can solve the problem of poverty in our lifetimes. In *The End of Poverty*, he cites examples of success in communities all over the developing world, showing what works in empowering communities and building foundations for prosperity.

We can absolutely replication and expand success, and poverty does not have to mean low achievement and expectations.

Examples of extraordinary success also exist here in Washington, DC, a district that is improving to become more competitive every year. For example, under a new principal at one school, student reading proficiency went from 24 percent to 85 percent in just four years, and from 10 percent to 64 percent in math. In another, only 9 percent of the students were on grade level, when just down the street in a successful charter school, over 90 percent of students were. Same kids, same neighborhoods and exposure to violence, same poverty, hunger, and parent education levels. At the successful schools, the primary difference was the team of adults who decided it was possible for lives and outcomes to move in other directions.

What is keeping us from bringing such examples to scale is not a lack of solutions but a frailty of belief. We can absolutely replicate and expand success, and poverty does not have to mean low achievement and expectations.

Changing the Way We See Poverty

I love the way Sachs described what it will take to end global poverty. Citing an experience in Western Kenya, he concluded a lecture on his book with a focus not on operational shifts but with a shift in our mindset.

We can end poverty, he said, "if we understand that we are dealing with people fighting for their lives . . . with people whose first objective is not to take our money but to see their children survive . . . with people that work harder than we can imagine to make something out of nothing . . . who in the midst of an AIDS pandemic, malaria endemic, and chronic hunger can put 37 out of 37 eighth graders through success on the 8th grade exam because they have that much social capital."

Education Must Come Before Politics

It will still take courage to change the beliefs that are keeping children and families in poverty. Many leaders are starting to show that courage, putting children before political interest in their decisions and policies, and preserving funding for education even when longstanding results will not come until years after the next election.

Nowhere is it more important than education to put politics last, and this is no easy feat.

For example, we have a Democratic president who is backing ideas (such as choice and competition) for their impact instead of the political party that claims them. President Obama is a huge supporter of charter schools and is letting competition drive the allocation of $4 billion in Race to the Top dollars he added to education. His administration is pledging to use it for districts introducing commonsense practices such as teacher assessment that includes student achievement—another idea he has not been afraid to embrace just because Republicans support it.

Nowhere is it more important than education to put politics last, and this is no easy feat. But I am encouraged by the ways it is happening nationally and in cities with courageous mayors who are prioritizing education. DC, New York, and Atlanta are showing results of this kind of leadership already, and I believe it is just the beginning.

For many individuals who work with children, courage will mean changing a long-standing mindset that has excused us from holding high expectations for all children. In the DC

Public Schools in 2007, performance evaluations had not been conducted for years in our central office, and teachers did not have clear guidelines about what we believed good teaching even looks like. Yet to educate all children well in any system, staff need the courage to participate in conversations about their performance that are tied to job security.

There is no doubt that poverty drags multiple obstacles into schools with children, and these obstacles are extremely challenging to overcome. It can feel like climbing a mountain every day, both for children and the adults who are teaching them. But there are successful mountain climbers. As we follow their examples in larger numbers, we will create well-worn paths of success. Mountains will be reduced to hills, and hills to level ground as all children become poised for life choices that can compete with their imaginations.

6

Is Education the Cure for Poverty?

Jared Bernstein

Jared Bernstein is an economist serving as Chief Economist and Economic Policy Adviser to Vice President Joseph Biden.

Education alone will not lift people out of poverty. While research supports the idea that targeted training for jobs and employment skills boost success, the real problem goes far beyond individual improvement. The combination of employment opportunity, work supports, and subsidies of the late 1990s are now eroding. The government must implement policies that allow those who invest in education and skills training to reap their fair share of economic rewards.

Economists may disagree a lot on policy, but we all agree on the "education premium"—the earnings boost associated with more education. But what role can education play in a realistic antipoverty policy agenda? And what are the limits of that role?

First, it depends on whether you're talking about children or adults, and schooling versus job training. And second, the extent to which education is rewarded depends on what else is going on in the economy.

As Greg J. Duncan's companion piece (page A20) [in "High quality Preschool as Antipoverty"] suggests, investment in early childhood has immense benefits. And at the other end of the schooling spectrum, college graduates' wage advantage over those with only a high-school diploma went up dramatically in the 1980s and early '90s. But the premium that high-school graduates enjoy over dropouts has been flat for decades. In 1973, high-school grads earned about 15.7 percent more per hour than dropouts, 15.9 percent in 1989, 16.1 percent in 2000, and 15.5 percent last year. And for adult workers, the historical record for job-training programs is pretty dismal, though more recent initiatives—with their focus on more carefully targeting training for local labor markets—show much more promise.

Nobody doubts that a better-educated workforce is more likely to enjoy higher earnings. But education by itself is a necessary insufficient antipoverty tool. Yes, poor people absolutely need more education and skill training but they also need an economic context wherein they can realize the economic returns from their improved human capital. Over the past few decades, the set of institutions and norms that historically maintained the link between skills and incomes have been diminished, particularly for non-college-educated workers. Restoring their strength and status is essential if we want the poor to reap the benefits they deserve from educational advancement.

What Research Shows

Julie Strawn of the Center for Law and Social Policy, reviewing an extensive sample of basic education and mining programs, concluded that education alone is much less successful in raising employment and earnings prospects than education combined with a strategy of focused job training (with an eye on local demand), "soft skills," and holding out for quality jobs.

One study found that a year of schooling raised the earnings of welfare recipients by 7 percent, the conventional labor economics finding. But given that many of these workers entered the job market in the $6- to $8-an-hour range back in the 1990s, you're talking about moving families closer to the poverty line, not pushing them significantly above it.

Strawn reports that when education is combined with multidimensional job training, readiness, and a quality job search, the returns more than double. One Portland, Oregon, program resulted in a 25 percent increase in earnings, a 21 percent increase in employment, and a 22 percent reduction of time spent on welfare (all compared with a control group that didn't get the services).

This finding makes intuitive sense: Programs that combine general education with training specific to both the individual and his or her local labor market work better than ones that fail to combine these activities. (They're also more expensive, but you get what you pay for.) Yet to get to the nub of the strengths and limits of education and poverty reduction, we need to go back to first principles and think about how they interact with the realities of the political economy.

A danger of overreliance on education in the poverty debate is that skilled workers end up all dressed up with nowhere nice to go.

Education is only a partial cure for poverty because of all the other recent changes in the labor market. At least half of the inequality increase has taken place within groups of comparably educated people, and since 2000 that proportion has been increasing. Income-inequality data show that the concentration of income in 2005 is the highest it has been since 1929. Yet research that Lawrence Mishel and I conducted shows that since the late 1990s, the college wage premium has been flat. In real terms, college wages were up less than 2 percent from 2000 to 2006. Even among the highly educated, only some are getting ahead, and lots aren't.

In short, we are not living in a meritocracy, where we can reliably count on people being fairly rewarded for their improved skills. So we need additional mechanisms in place to nudge the invisible hand toward outcomes that are more meritocratic and just.

Skill Demands for the Working Poor

Education is a supply-side policy; it improves the quality of workers, not the quality or the quantity of jobs. A danger of overreliance on education in the poverty debate is that skilled workers end up all dressed up with nowhere nice to go.

Some economists contend that faster rates of technological advance require ever more highly skilled workers, and that demand shifts lead to low wages for the low skilled. But our work at the Economic Policy Institute suggests that while technological changes have always been an important factor in the labor market, the rate of change now is no greater than in the recent past. Technological change is one of the reasons we've doubled the share of college grads but continued to see their unemployment rates in the 2 percent range—we produce and absorb a lot of college grads.

Our economy, however, is still very much structured to produce lots of low-wage jobs. In fact, according to the occupational projections by the Bureau of Labor Statistics, the low-wage sector of our economy will be the source of much job growth over the next decade. The American economy will continue to employ significant numbers of retail salespersons, waiters and waitresses, food-prep workers, home health aides, maids and housekeepers, etc. Of the 30 occupations adding the most jobs to our economy, those requiring the least training make up half of the total.

The question, thus, is not whether jobs for those with only high-school degrees or even some college will exist or be plentiful in our future (they almost certainly will be); the question is whether the quality of these jobs will help reduce or reinforce working poverty.

In our most recent version of "The State of Working America," we borrow a technique from economist Sheldon Danziger and Peter Gottschalk for analyzing the roles played by multiple determinants of poverty. Their method parses out the roles of race, family structure, economic growth, and inequality, and we add the role of education.

. . . Family poverty rates did not fall much between 1969 and 2000, because major factors were offsetting one another. Improved education lowered family poverty by almost 4 percentage points, a considerable effect. But economic growth and inequality had considerably larger effects. Growth in the overall economy lowered poverty rates by 5.7 points, while inequality raised it by 5.1 points. Family structure added 3 points to family poverty rates over these years, and race added 1 point.

Decompositions of this type are far from definitive; they tend to hold one factor constant and see how things change, then do the same for another factor, etc. But in this case, the results are demonstrative of the main point regarding education in the poverty debate: It's an important part of the story, but it's not the whole story, or even the most important part.

Education Plus

Demand—the extent of overall growth, how taut the labor market is—matters, as does the extent and nature of inequality, as does the quality of jobs. In the late 1990s, poverty fell to historic lows for those with the lowest education levels, including African Americans and single mothers. Did skills rain from the heavens? Did employers suddenly shed their advanced-skill requirements? Of course not. It was good old-fashioned full employment forcing employers to bid wages up to get—and keep—the workers they needed. And yes, this interacted with welfare reform and a significant expansion of work supports, like the Earned Income Tax Credit, subsidized health and child care, and the minimum-wage increase.

In fact, one could be forgiven for thinking that, except for some of the punitive aspects of welfare reform, we briefly got poverty reduction right during the late 1990s. The one-two punch of full employment and expanded work supports worked to meet the expanding labor supply with even faster growing labor demand, and the subsidies helped to close part of the gap between what people earned and what they needed.

Workers need a context wherein they can be rewarded for their skills.

But notice how all of this is unwinding in the 2000s. Un-employment is low, but other indicators—such as labor-force participation and real wage trends—suggest we're not yet at full employment; there's been no expansion of work supports, and even some retrenchment of supports such as the State Children's Health Insurance Program and child care, policies clearly associated with helping the working poor get ahead. The outcome has been predictable and depressing, especially in contrast to the progress we made in the 1990s.

And if education is one key antipoverty strategy, then programs demanding that beneficiaries "work first" often sacrifice the promise of increased returns to education and training on the altar of take-any-job. This approach is not only stingy; it's also shortsighted, as it threatens to diminish the likelihood that those who want to "play by the rules" will realize their economic potential.

Helping the poor receive more education is part of the answer. Whatever their skill level, workers need a context wherein they can be rewarded for their skills, where the benefits of the growth they help to create flow freely their way. This means having a set of protections, institutions, regulations, and social norms in place to keep the greedy fingers of inequality from picking the pockets of the working poor.

7

Marriage Reduces Poverty

Robert Rector

Robert Rector is Senior Research Fellow in the Domestic Policy Studies Department at the Heritage Foundation.

Marriage is the single best anti-poverty tool society has. Statistics show that the absence of married fathers in the home leads to inferior life outcomes for children. Contrary to left-wing belief, the decline of marriage among low-income populations is not due to teen pregnancy, issues around birth control, or unwanted births. Instead, low income individuals tend to see marriage as a lofty goal, something that needs to be put off rather than the path to reach their goals. America must encourage pro-marriage policies in order to win the battle against poverty.

The mainstream media, liberal politicians, activists, and academia bewail child poverty in the U.S. But in these ritual lamentations, one key fact remains hidden: The principal cause of child poverty in the U.S. is the absence of married fathers in the home.

According to the U.S Census, the poverty rate in 2008 for single parents with children was 35.6 percent. The rate for married couples with children was 6.4 percent. Being raised in a married family reduces a child's probability of living in poverty by about 80 percent.

True, some of this difference in poverty is due to the fact that single parents tend to have less education than married

Robert Rector, "Married Fathers: America's Greatest Weapon Against Child Poverty," The Heritage Foundation, June 16, 2010. Copyright © 2010 The Heritage Foundation. Reproduced by permission.

couples. But even when married couples are compared to single parents with the same education level, the married poverty rate will still be about 70 percent lower.

Marriage is a powerful weapon in fighting poverty. In fact, being married has the same effect in reducing poverty as adding five to six years to a parent's education level.

The U.S. is steadily separating into a two-caste system, with marriage and education as the dividing line.

A Two-Caste Society

Unfortunately, marriage is rapidly declining in American society. When President Lyndon Johnson launched the War on Poverty in 1963, 93 percent of American children were born to married parents. Today the number has dropped to 59 percent.

In 2008, 1.7 million children were born outside marriage. As noted, most of these births occurred to women who will have the hardest time going it alone as parents: young adult women with a high school degree or less. College-educated women rarely have children outside marriage.

The U.S. is steadily separating into a two-caste system, with marriage and education as the dividing line. In the high-income third of the population, children are raised by married parents with a college education; in the bottom-income third, children are raised by single parents with a high school degree or less. Single parents now comprise 70 percent of all poor families with children. Last year, government provided over $300 billion in means-tested welfare aid to single parents.

The Lifelong Effects of Fathers

The positive effects of married fathers are not limited to income alone. Children raised by married parents have substantially better life outcomes compared to similar children raised in single-parent homes. When compared to children in intact married homes, children raised by single parents are more likely to have emotional and behavioral problems; be physically abused; smoke, drink, and use drugs; be aggressive; engage in violent, delinquent, and criminal behavior; have poor school performance; be expelled from school; and drop out of high school. Many of these negative outcomes are associated with the higher poverty rates of single mothers. But, in many cases, the improvements in child well-being associated with marriage persist even after adjusting for differences in family income. This indicates that the father brings more to his home than just a paycheck.

The effect of married fathers on child outcomes can be quite pronounced. For example, examination of families with the same race and same parental education shows that, when compared to intact married families, children from single-parent homes are:

- More than twice as likely to be arrested for a juvenile crime;

- Twice as likely to be treated for emotional and behavioral problems;

- Roughly twice as likely to be suspended or expelled from school; and

- A third more likely to drop out before completing high school.

The effects of being raised in a single-parent home continue into adulthood. Comparing families of the same race and similar incomes, children from broken and single-parent homes are three times more likely to end up in jail by the time they reach age 30 than are children raised in intact married families. Compared to girls raised in similar married families, girls from single-parent homes are more than twice as likely to have a child without being married, thereby repeating the negative cycle for another generation.

Finally, the decline of marriage generates poverty in future generations. Children living in single parent homes are 50 percent more likely to experience poverty as adults when compared to children from intact married homes. This intergenerational poverty effect persists even after adjusting for the original differences in family income and poverty during childhood.

If poor single mothers were married to the actual fathers of their children, two-thirds would immediately be lifted out of poverty.

The Left's Misdiagnosis

Marriage matters. But mentioning the bond between marriage and lower poverty violates the protocols of political correctness. Thus, the main cause of child poverty remains hidden from public view. And even when the Left reluctantly mentions the decline of marriage in low-income communities, most of what they say about it is untrue. For example,

- Liberals insist that poor women become pregnant outside marriage because they lack knowledge about, and access to, birth control. In fact, virtually no non-marital pregnancies in low-income communities occur for that reason.

- Liberals insist that the main problem in low-income communities is "teen pregnancy." In fact, only 8 percent of all out-of-wedlock births occur to teens under 18; most occur to young adult women in their 20s.

- Liberals insist that most out-of-wedlock pregnancies and births are accidental. In fact, most women who give birth out of wedlock strongly desire children. Their pregnancies are partially intended or at least not seriously avoided.

The Left also argues that poor single mothers do not marry because the fathers of their children lack jobs, income, and are largely "non-marriageable." This also is untrue: Nearly all non-married fathers are employed at the time their children are born. Most have higher earnings than the mothers. In fact, if poor single mothers were married to the actual fathers of their children, two-thirds would immediately be lifted out of poverty.

Finally, the Left argues that poor mothers and fathers are uninterested in marriage. Research by Harvard sociologist Kathryn Edin shows the opposite. Low-income men and women greatly value marriage and aspire to be married. However, they no longer believe it is important to be married before having children. They idealize marriage, viewing it the same way the upper middle class might view a trip to Paris: an event that would be wonderful in the future but is not necessary or important at the present time. While the upper middle class get married first and then have children, the poor follow the opposite path; they have children first and then look for suitable partner to help raise them.

Edin's research shows that most poor single mothers have traditional life goals. They want a house in the suburbs, two kids, a husband, a minivan, and a dog. But they fail to understand the importance of marriage to achieving these goals. They see marriage as a symbolic ceremony that should occur in middle age, a celebration of one's successful entry into the middle class. They do not appreciate that for most families in the middle class, marriage is a necessary pathway to financial stability and prosperity, rather than a symbolic event that comes after prosperity is achieved.

What Government Should—and Should Not—Do

To reinvigorate marriage in lower-income communities, government could provide factual information on the role of healthy marriages in reducing poverty and improving child well-being. It could explain why it is important to develop a stable marital relationship before bringing children into the world. It could teach skills for selecting potential life partners and building stable relationships.

Historically, the Left has been indifferent or hostile to marriage. For decades, feminists actually taught that marriage harmed women psychologically and economically.

But nothing could be farther from actual government practice. In social service agencies, welfare offices, schools, and popular culture in low-income communities across America, one finds deafening silence on the topic of marriage. The welfare system actively penalizes low-income couples who do marry.

The gag rule about marriage is nothing new. At the beginning of the War on Poverty, a young Daniel Patrick Moynihan (later Ambassador to the United Nations and Senator from New York), serving in the Administration of President Lyndon Johnson, wrote a seminal report on the negative effects of declining marriage among blacks. The Left exploded, excoriating Moynihan and insisting that the erosion of marriage was either unimportant or benign.

Four decades later, Moynihan's predictions have been vindicated. The erosion of marriage has spread to whites and Hispanics with devastating results. But the taboo on discussing the link between poverty and the disappearance of husbands remains as firm as it was four decades ago.

Historically, the Left has been indifferent or hostile to marriage. For decades, feminists actually taught that marriage harmed women psychologically and economically. While few would accept those ideas literally anymore, an instinctive hostility to marriage remains imprinted on the synapses of most liberal academics. In most faculty lounges, enthusiasm for marriage would be quite gauche [not tactful].

For most on the Left, marriage is, at best, an antiquated institution, a red-state superstition. From this viewpoint, the real task is to expand government subsidies as a post-marriage society is built. Given this backdrop, it is not surprising that the Obama Administration seeks to abolish the one existing government program aimed at strengthening marriage in low-income communities: the miniscule Healthy Marriage Initiative operated through the Department of Health and Human Services.

Marriage: The Antidote to Poverty

Despite the politically correct gag rule, marriage remains America's strongest anti-poverty weapon. Unfortunately, marriage continues to decline. As husbands disappear from the home, poverty and welfare dependence will increase. Children and parents will suffer as a result.

Since the decline of marriage is the principal cause of child poverty and welfare dependence in the U.S., and since the poor aspire to healthy marriage but lack the norms, understanding, and skills to achieve it, it would seem reasonable for government to take steps to strengthen marriage. In particular, clarifying the severe shortcomings of the "child first, marriage later" philosophy to potential parents in lower-income communities would seem to be a priority.

To reduce poverty in America, policymakers should enact policies that encourage people to form and maintain healthy marriage and delay childbearing until they are married and economically stable. Marriage is highly beneficial to children, adults, and society. It needs to be encouraged and strengthened, not ignored and undermined.

8

Marriage Is Not the Answer to Poverty

Polly Toynbee

Polly Toynbee, an author and journalist, writes a column for the Guardian, *a British newspaper.*

In the United Kingdom, the Conservative Party's misguided view that marriage is the cure for poverty has been reinforced by a recent partisan survey. The theory ignores issues of disenfranchisement and women's salary inequality and instead moralizes the lives of hardworking citizens. Being a single mother may not be ideal but it is often the reality, and marriage is not the answer for everyone at any income level. By continuing this line of reasoning, the Conservatives fail to endorse policies—like the minimum wage and tax credits—that will actually help alleviate poverty.

Miserable Conservatives dazed and confused by their leader's strange sayings and doings can heave a sigh of relief. A report on poverty from Iain Duncan Smith's Social Justice group takes the party back to good solid Tory [the Tory Party, or Tories, are other names for the Conservative Party in the United Kingdom] terra firma [ground]. What are the causes of poverty? The poor. What would help cure them of their afflictions? Marriage. Yesterday he blamed Five Pathways to Poverty—family breakdown, educational failure, economic dependence, indebtedness and addiction. Conservative associations up and down the land will nod in happy agreement. Remoralising the poor and giving them higher aspirations is the answer to their plight—and indeed some of his proposals are excellent. But, though his policy group calls itself Social Justice, not a word here concerns the yawning inequality between the top and the bottom. Asked about that, Duncan Smith hastens to say they were only concerned with saving those at the bottom from themselves.

Mothers can rarely earn enough to lift their families out of poverty. But don't expect an analysis of why women's work is so badly paid.

With over 300,000 words in seven volumes, it is good news that at last the Tories are taking the facts of poverty seriously. Even though Oliver Letwin's pledge to endorse Labour's promise to abolish child poverty by 2020 was later downgraded to an "aspiration", it means that, if they regain power,[1] they will at least be embarrassed if child poverty soars as it did last time (from one child in nine in 1979 to one in three by the time they left office). That is progress.

The Real Causes of Poverty

But this torrent of facts mainly reciting the blindingly obvious has a gigantic logical nonsense at its heart. Its arguments are circular, confusing causes and effects, citing symptoms as if they were reasons. Take their headline message—marriage. The facts do indeed show that single parenthood makes many families destitute. Mothers can rarely earn enough to lift their families out of poverty. But don't expect an analysis of why women's work is so badly paid. Instead, here are the figures showing how the children of broken homes are more likely to fail at school and be unemployed, drug-addicted, mentally ill

1. In May 11, 2010 Conservative Party Leader David Cameron became Prime Minister. The Conservative Party also regained Parliament (in coalition with the Liberal Democrats).

or in jail. That poverty causes separation or that poor mothers throw out fathers who can't earn, or who are themselves addicts or criminals in a blighted world of deprivation doesn't feature much. Instead, a great leap into logical fallacy concludes that lack of a marriage certificate is the prime cause of all the rest.

Let's get one thing straight, since critics of this magical view of marriage are accused of promoting single motherhood. Everyone agrees that children stand the best chance with two loving parents who stay together happily. It's what most parents want, but many fail to achieve. Cohabitees are less likely to stay together than married parents, but it is a leap to conclude that marriage magically glues parents together. People who marry are different, for all kinds of social and emotional reasons. Driving cohabitees to the altar is unlikely to change anything. And how would it be done?

Issues of Enforcing a Moral Agenda

Since parents face heavy losses on divorce, how could the state impose stronger financial incentives to stay together? Draconian [extreme, harsh] action could let single mothers and children starve on the streets without benefits to deter others, but the government would fall long before there was any shift in the moral culture. This is not just back to basics, but back to the old realms of Tory fantasy social policy. John Gummer proposed putting single mothers into hostels as a disincentive to pregnancy but the idea was dropped, as it would cost as much as keeping them in prison. It's odd how the small-government party dreams of impossible governmental power when it comes to moral matters.

Duncan Smith protests that the benefit system favours single parenthood, since a couple draws less in credits or benefits than if the adults lived apart. Would they redress this by giving both parents the same benefits, regardless of joint income? It would cost £17bn, if joint income was disregarded altogether—almost enough to abolish child poverty anyway. They could, of course, cut benefits for single parents to pay for it—but that would impose real punishment.

The Tories ignore the working poor altogether, beyond bemoaning tax credits and means testing, happier by far to focus on "Shameless" families instead.

Marriage Incentives Will Not Benefit the Poor

Supporting marriage financially is one of David Cameron's few firm policies. His marriage tax incentive would give non-working wives a right to a tax allowance, transferrable for use against their husband's earnings. It might influence a few better-off couples to marry, but it would pay huge sums to the already married, a vast dead-weight cost. All the gainers would be higher earners. With tax credits, poor parents don't pay tax and certainly not enough to deduct two personal allowances from one salary. This is redistribution to the well-off without giving extra to anyone near the poverty line, however married they are.

Marriage is the headline but, underneath it all, here are the outlines of real Tory intentions. These documents lay siege to the policy that has done most to lift children out of poverty—tax credits. They castigate the government for subjecting many more families to means testing, without mentioning the reason—the hundreds of thousands now receiving much more money. The accelerating attacks on tax credits suggest that the Tories are preparing the way to cutting them. They call them "dependency" and label them as a cause of poverty instead of part of the remedy.

Good Social Policy Is Needed

Tax credits are indeed a problem: why should the taxpayer subsidise low-paying employers? But naturally the party that opposed the minimum wage does not draw the obvious conclusion—that if earnings rose there would be no need for state subsidy. Nowhere does this report recognise that most of the poor are not dysfunctional. Most are in work, doing essential jobs that society depends on, yet still not earning enough to keep a family. Labour finds that hard to discuss but at least it brought in a minimum wage and tax credits to fill the gap. The Tories ignore the working poor altogether, beyond bemoaning tax credits and means testing, happier by far to focus on "Shameless" families instead.

Marriage is the Tories' happy hunting ground, their comfort zone. It may hearten their heartland, but its wider political value is doubtful. Most ordinary families have divorce in their midst and they know life is complicated. It is a genuine social problem that a quarter of children live in single-parent families, yet society still fails to let mothers support a family. But as for cause and effect, one fact is conveniently missing from these reports: Denmark has exactly the same proportion of one-parent families and the least child poverty in the EU [European Union]. Good social policy trumps moralising.

9

Raising the Minimum Wage Will Help the Poor

Holly Sklar

An op-ed columnist and author, Holly Sklar serves as a Senior Policy Advisor for the Let Justice Roll Living Wage Campaign.

Raising the minimum wage is not only important for poverty reduction, but also as a means of providing economic stimulus during the worst economic downturn since the Great Depression. Minimum wage workers put their increased income directly back into the economy in order to meet their basic needs. Far from leading to unemployment, approving a living wage will lift individuals out of poverty and the economy out of crisis.

Summary

- The federal minimum wage was enacted during the Great Depression to promote economic recovery.

- The long-term fall in worker buying power is a key reason we are in the worst economic crisis since the Great Depression.

- An America that doesn't work for working people is not an America that works.

- Raising the minimum wage boosts consumer purchasing power and economic recovery.

Holly Sklar, "Raising the Minimum Wage in Hard Times," Let Justice Roll Living Wage Campaign, July 22, 2009. Reproduced by permission.

- Raising the minimum wage does not increase unemployment in good times or bad.

- Raise the floor to lift the economy.

A growing share of workers make too little to buy necessities—much less afford a middle-class standard of living.

The Federal Minimum Wage Was Enacted During the Great Depression to Promote Economic Recovery

The federal minimum wage was not enacted during good times, but during the extraordinarily hard times of the Great Depression.[1] When the federal minimum wage was established in 1938, the unemployment rate was still a very high 19 percent.

President Franklin Roosevelt called the minimum wage "an essential part of economic recovery." It would put a floor under worker wages, alleviate the hardship of inadequate wages, and stimulate the economy and job creation by increasing consumer purchasing power. The federal minimum wage was also meant to promote economic development and stop the original "race to the bottom" of employers moving to cheaper labor states in a downward spiral.

In his January 3, 1938 annual message to Congress, calling for passage of the historic Fair Labor Standards Act, Roosevelt said, millions of workers "receive pay so low that they have little buying power. Aside from the undoubted fact that they thereby suffer great human hardship, they are unable to buy adequate food and shelter, to maintain health or to buy their share of manufactured goods."

1. For a good overview, see Jonathan Grossman, "Fair Labor Standards Act of 1938: Maximum Struggle for a Minimum Wage," U.S. Department of Labor, http://www.dol.gov/oasam/programs/history/flsa1938.htm. Also see Kirstin Downey, *The Woman Behind the New Deal: The Life of Frances Perkins, FDR's Secretary of Labor and His Moral Conscience* (New York: Doubleday, 2009).

Roosevelt said, "The increase of national purchasing power [is] an underlying necessity of the day." And so it is today.

The Long-Term Fall in Worker Buying Power Is a Key Reason We Are in the Worst Economic Crisis Since the Great Depression

Consumer spending makes up about 70% of our economy. The minimum wage sets the wage floor. A low minimum wage institutionalizes an increasingly low-wage workforce and undermines our economy.

The decade between the federal minimum wage increases on Sept. 1, 1997 and July 24, 2007 was the longest period in history without a raise. Minimum wage increases have been so little, so late that today's $7.25 minimum wage is lower than the inflation-adjusted $8.03 minimum wage of 1956—more than 50 years ago. The minimum wage reached its peak value in 1968. It would take a $10.04 minimum wage to match the buying power of the minimum wage in 1968.

A growing share of workers make too little to buy necessities—much less afford a middle-class standard of living. More and more two-paycheck households struggle to afford a home, college, healthcare and retirement once characteristic of middle-class households on one paycheck.

There has been a massive shift of income from the bottom and middle to the top. In 1973, the richest 1% of Americans had 9% of the nation's income. By 2007—leading in to the Great Recession—the richest 1% of Americans had increased their share of the nation's income to 23.5%. That nearly tied the record 23.9% in 1928—on the eve of the Great Depression.

- Average wages are 7% percent lower today, adjusted for inflation, than they were in 1973.

- The IRS [Internal Revenue Service] has reported on the 400 taxpayers with the highest incomes since 1992. Between 1992 and 2007, adjusting for inflation, the 400 highest-income taxpayers increased their average income by 399%.

As we are seeing so painfully, an economy fueled by rising debt, greed and speculation, rather than rising wages and productive investment, is a house of cards.

"When businesses don't pay a living wage all society pays," said U.S. Women's Chamber of Commerce CEO Margot Dorfman in signing a statement by national business leaders and small business owners from every state supporting the minimum wage increase passed in 2007. "We pay through poverty and needless disease, disability and death from inadequate healthcare. We pay as women struggle to put food on the table. We pay as businesses and communities suffer economic decline." (www.businessforafairminimumwage.org)

An America That Doesn't Work for Working People Is Not an America That Works

Let Justice Roll predicted the economic meltdown in our first report, *A Just Minimum Wage: Good for Workers, Business and Our Future*, in 2005. We called for an end to the low-wage, low-social responsibility low road, saying, "The high road is not only the better road, it is the only road for progress in the future. An America that doesn't work for working people is not an America that works. We will not prosper economically or ethically in the global economy relying on low wages, outsourcing and debt in place of innovation and opportunity. We will not prosper in the global economy relying on disinvestment in place of reinvestment. We can't succeed that way any more than farmers can 'compete' by eating their seed corn."

We said, "The United States is an increasingly shaky superpower with a hollowed-out manufacturing base, large trade deficit and growing debt held heavily by other countries.

Households have propped themselves up in the face of falling real wages by maxing out work hours, credit cards and home equity loans . . . This is not a sustainable course . . . The low road is like a 'shortcut' that leads to a cliff."

We have fallen off the cliff.

Underpaid workers and responsible businesses have been bailing out banks and corporations run by reckless overpaid bosses who milked their companies and our country like cash cows–and trashed the global economy. Enough is enough.

Minimum wage workers don't put raises into Wall Street's many Ponzi schemes, commodity speculation or offshore tax havens.

Raising the Minimum Wage Boosts Consumer Purchasing Power and Economic Recovery

We hear a lot of talk about the importance of consumer spending to recovery from our current economic crisis. Well, consumers can't spend what they don't have. If consumer purchasing power is at the heart of economic recovery, wages are at the heart of consumer purchasing power.

Minimum wage workers, like all workers, are also consumers. Minimum wage raises are well-targeted for economic recovery because they go directly to those who most need to spend additional dollars on food, fuel, housing, healthcare and other necessities.

Minimum wage workers don't put raises into Wall Street's many Ponzi schemes, commodity speculation or offshore tax havens. They recycle their raises back into local businesses and the economy by buying needed goods and services.

According to the Economic Policy Institute report, *A Stealthy Stimulus: How boosting the minimum wage is helping to stimulate the economy,* the first two minimum wage increases "will have generated an estimated $4.9 billion of spending by July 2009, precisely when our economy needed it the most. The final increase in July 2009 is expected to generate another $5.5 billion over the following year."

Raising the Minimum Wage Does Not Increase Unemployment in Good Times or Bad

Critics routinely oppose minimum wage increases in good times and bad, claiming they will increase unemployment, no matter the real world record to the contrary. Extensive research refutes the claim that increasing the minimum wage causes increased unemployment and business closures. Key national, state and citywide studies appear in the Appendix.

The buying power of the minimum wage reached its peak in 1968. The unemployment rate went from 3.8% in 1967 to 3.6% in 1968 to 3.5% in 1969. The next time the unemployment rate came close to those levels was after the minimum wage raises of 1996 and 1997.

As *Business Week* put it in 2001, "Many economists have backed away from the argument that minimum wage [laws] lead to fewer jobs."

The decade between the federal minimum wage increase to $5.15 an hour on Sept. 1, 1997 and the July 24, 2007 increase to $5.85 was the longest period in history without a raise. Numerous states raised their minimum wages higher than the federal level during that period. Research by the Fiscal Policy Institute and others showed that states that raised minimum wages above the federal level experienced better employment and small business trends than states that did not.

A series of rigorous studies by the Institute for Research on Labor and Employment at the University of California, Berkeley, significantly advances the research on minimum wage employment effects. *Minimum Wage Effects Across State*

Borders compared all neighboring counties in the U.S. located on different sides of a state border with different minimum wage levels between 1990 and 2006. It found no adverse employment effects from higher minimum wages. The Institute's *Spacial Heterogeneity and Minimum Wages: Employment Estimates for Teens Using Cross-State Commuting Zones* found "no discernable disemployment effect, even when minimum wage increases lead to relatively large wage changes." *Do Minimum Wages Really Reduce Teen Employment?* analyzed the 1990-2009 period (an earlier version analyzed 1990-2007). Carefully controlling for more factors than previous minimum wage studies, the researchers found the answer is no.

Raise the Floor to Lift the Economy

The minimum wage sets the wage floor. As Roosevelt and his advisers understood, we have to raise the floor to lift the economy.

Frances Perkins was Secretary of Labor from 1933 to 1945 and the first woman to serve in a presidential cabinet. She accepted the position after securing Roosevelt's commitment to champion the minimum wage, a 40-hour workweek, unemployment insurance, Social Security and other hallmarks of the New Deal. In 1933, while still serving as Industrial Commissioner of the New York State Department of Labor, Perkins wrote in the magazine, *Survey Graphic,* about the real "cost of a five-dollar dress":

> It hangs in the window of one of the little cash-and-carry stores that now line a street where fashionable New Yorkers used to drive out in their carriages to shop at Tiffany's and Constable's. It is a "supper dress" of silk crepe in "the new red" ... A cardboard tag on the shoulder reads: "Special $4.95." Bargain basements and little ready-to-wear shops are filled with similar "specials."

But the manufacturer who pays a living wage for a reasonable week's work under decent conditions cannot turn out attractive silk frocks to retail at $5 or less ...

If the purchaser does not pay a price that allows for a subsistence wage and reasonable hours and working conditions, then the cost of the "bargain" must be sweated out of the workers.

The red silk bargain dress in the shop window is a danger signal. It is a warning of the return of the sweatshop, a challenge to us all to reinforce the gains we have made in our long and difficult progress towards a civilized industrial order.

Perkins wanted the minimum wage to be a living wage. The Department of Labor is located in the Frances Perkins Building. It's time to stop undoing Perkins' legacy and build on it.

Public opinion has long supported raising the minimum wage. The 2010 American Values Survey finds that 67% of the public supports increasing the minimum wage from $7.25 an hour to $10.

Paying workers enough to live on should not be optional—in good times or bad.

Appendix: Research Shows Raising Minimum Wage Does Not Increase Unemployment

Selected Research in Chronological Order

Lawrence F. Katz and Alan B. Krueger, "The Effect of the Minimum Wage on the Fast Food Industry," Industrial Relations Section, Princeton University, February 1992.

David Card, "Using Regional Variation in Wages to Measure the Effects of the Federal Minimum Wage," *Industrial and Labor Relations Review*, October 1992.

David Card and Alan Krueger, *Myth and Measurement: The New Economics of the Minimum Wage* (Princeton, NJ: Princeton University Press, 1995).

David Card and Alan B. Krueger, "Minimum Wages and Employment: A Case Study of the Fast-Food Industry in New Jersey and Pennsylvania: Reply," *American Economic Review*, December 2000 (in this reply, Card and Krueger update earlier findings and refute critics).

Jared Bernstein and John Schmitt, Economic Policy Institute, *Making Work Pay: The Impact of the 1996-97 Minimum Wage Increase*, 1998.

Jerold Waltman, Allan McBride and Nicole Camhout, "Minimum Wage Increases and the Business Failure Rate," *Journal of Economic Issues*, March 1998.

A Report by the National Economic Council, *The Minimum Wage: Increasing the Reward for Work*, March 2000.

Holly Sklar, Laryssa Mykyta and Susan Wefald, *Raise The Floor: Wages and Policies That Work For All Of Us* (Boston: South End Press, 2001/2002), Ch. 4 and pp. 102-08.

Marilyn P. Watkins, Economic Opportunity Institute, "Still Working Well: Washingtons Minimum Wage and the Beginnings of Economic Recovery," January 21, 2004.

Amy Chasanov, Economic Policy Institute, *No Longer Getting By: An Increase in the Minimum Wage is Long Overdue*, May 2004.

Fiscal Policy Institute, *States with Minimum Wages above the Federal Level Have Had Faster Small Business and Retail Job Growth*, March 2006 (update of 2004 report).

John Burton and Amy Hanauer, Center for American Progress and Policy Matters Ohio, *Good for Business: Small Business Growth and State Minimum Wages*, May 2006.

Paul K. Sonn, *Citywide Minimum Wage Laws: A New Policy Tool for Local Governments*, (originally published by Brennan Center for Justice) National Employment Law Project, May 2006, includes a good summary of impact research.

Liana Fox, Economic Policy Institute, *Minimum Wage Trends: Understanding past and contemporary research*, November 8, 2006.

Paul Wolfson, Economic Policy Institute, *State Minimum Wages: A Policy That Works*, November 27, 2006.

Arindrajit Dube, Suresh Naidu and Michael Reich, "The Economic Effects of a Citywide Minimum Wage," *Industrial & Industrial Labor Relations Review*, July 2007.

Jerold L. Waltman, *Minimum Wage Policy in Great Britain and the United States* (New York: Algora, 2008), pp. 17-19, 132-136, 151-162, 178-180.

Sylvia Allegretto, Arindrajit Dube and Michael Reich, *Do Minimum Wages Really Reduce Teen Employment?*, Institute for Research on Labor and Employment, Univ. of CA, Berkeley, June 28, 2008.

Arindrajit Dube, T. William Lester and Michael Reich, *Minimum Wage Effects Across State Borders: Estimates Using Contiguous Counties*, Institute for Research on Labor and Employment, Univ. of CA, Berkeley, August 2008.

Michael F. Thompson, Indiana Business Research Center, "Minimum Wage Impacts on Employment: A Look at Indiana, Illinois and Surrounding Midwestern States," *Indiana Business Review*, Fall 2008.

Sylvia Allegretto, Arindrajit Dube and Michael Reich, *Spacial Heterogeneity and Minimum Wages: Employment Estimates for Teens Using Cross-State Commuting Zones*, Institute for Research on Labor and Employment, Univ. of CA, Berkeley, June 25, 2009.

Sylvia Allegretto, Arindrajit Dube and Michael Reich, *Do Minimum Wages Really Reduce Teen Employment? Accounting for Heterogeneity and Selectivity in State Panel Data*, Institute for Research on Labor and Employment, Univ. of CA, Berkeley, June 21, 2010.

10

Wage Regulation Will Not Help the Poor

Bill Barnes

Bill Barnes studied economics at the University of Georgia and is a business development representative for IDS Links.

Mandating a living wage would hurt the very people it's supposed to help. Any perceived benefits of this policy ignore the the larger economic picture. Forcing employers to pay more for employees than their skills are worth would result in increased unemployment. The resulting joblessness would increase crime. Low-wage employment improves job skills for workers and keeps low cost goods and services available for everyone.

Athens, Georgia, is widely considered to be impoverished. A "living wage" is usually the result of a local government effort to increase the legally permissible wage above the state or federally mandated minimum wage in that area.

Many residents of Athens have been trying to implement a living wage in the community for some time. These efforts are largely supported by the faculty, staff, and students at the University of Georgia, in Athens. Focusing on some of the least-skilled workers, I show why the living wage would not have any positive impact on the poor in Athens and why a higher mandated wage could further impoverish them.

There are plenty of people who can tell you the "benefits" of a living wage. Of course, these benefits are very shallow and

Bill Barnes, "The Illusion of Living Wage Laws," *Mises Daily*, October 15, 2009. Reproduced by permission.

short-term. A deeper economic and social analysis demonstrates the appalling costs of such regulation.

Living Wage Effect on Unemployment

As with all government regulations, the most significant problem with living-wage legislation would be the unforeseen consequences, in this case unemployment. Many would say that unemployment levels do not increase very much when living-wage laws are enacted, but looking at general employment numbers does little for determining the effects on the poor.

Take, for instance, current unemployment statistics in Georgia. Unemployment in the state has hovered between 3.4 and 6.5 percent over the past decade. These rates are deemed acceptable by our government and it is unlikely that they are much affected by the minimum wage. Additionally, based on other states' experiences, one would not anticipate a large change in the unemployment rate due to living-wage legislation.

However, I contend that the small magnitude of changes in the general unemployment rate does not justify a living wage because it does not represent its impact on the poor. Poor people make up a small fraction of the people counted by employment measures.

A change in the generally reported unemployment rates does not reflect the changes many poor (or less-skilled/inexperienced) people feel.

The overwhelming majority of Americans in the workforce are not directly affected by living-wage laws. Their jobs are safe because they are worth significantly more to their employers than any (current) mandated wages. If we want to discuss the effects of the living wage among the poor, we must consider only the poor in our statistics.

Effects on Teenagers and Unskilled Workers

Let us consider some of the less-employable American workers: teenagers. Teenagers are generally worth lower wages than any other age group in society, due to their immaturity and lack of experience. Indeed, it stands to reason that people are worth the least in the first job they ever take. Typically, the best teenage workers' wages will increase during the first few years. Most, however, will not see any significant wage increases until they finish school or move into full-time work.

The unemployment rate is measured as a percentage: people who want work but cannot find it are divided into the total number of people who want work, including those who are actively in the workforce. According to US Department of Labor statistics, American teenagers experienced an unemployment rate of 15.7 percent in 2007. (Note that this low figure was during the Fed-fueled boom). This is one group of people who truly are affected by living-wage legislation. A change in the generally reported unemployment rates does not reflect the changes many poor (or less-skilled/inexperienced) people feel.

This number would be very susceptible to a change in mandated minimum wages because so many teenagers are already worth barely more than the current minimum wage in terms of productivity per hour. Whether it is poor teenagers or other unskilled groups, higher wage laws are only going to decrease their opportunities to find work and improve job skills.

Clearly, some people are going to be adversely affected by a living wage. One could argue from a standpoint of liberty (formerly an American ideal), that laws adversely affecting some groups should not be enacted, but we will only look at the economic impacts of such legislation here.

The data show that the people most likely to be affected by living-wage legislation are black, teenage males. This group had a national unemployment rate of 33.8 percent in 2007.

When the data are broken down for black males aged 16 and 17, the unemployment rate is in excess of 40 percent.

These numbers are staggering, and they would only get worse with a living wage. Some teenagers would not even have the option of work because the value of their marginal revenue would not equal their new, higher wage cost.

So, what happens to these people who are left jobless? Well, they still need money and something to do during the day.

Due to the higher mandated wage, jobs that are not worth this wage will no longer be performed legally in the community.

Not surprisingly, crime rates are highest among those in their late teens and early twenties. The Georgia Bureau of Investigation cites young people, aged 17–21, as perpetrating 23.4 percent of the crimes in the state.

It is no coincidence that those who cannot find work tend to find things that get them into trouble to fill their time. I argue that enactment of a living wage would only put more young people on the streets rather than in jobs where they can learn skills that will serve them well in the future.

A Decrease in Available Services

Not only is this lack of work bad for young people and other low-skilled workers, but it also hurts the local economy. Due to the higher mandated wage, jobs that are not worth this wage will no longer be performed legally in the community. Trash pickup, general cleaning, inexpensive food preparation, farming, and many other tasks would be either neglected or moved to places with lower wage costs.

This general lack of production would not be due to people's lack of desire to do the work, but to government's intervention, which would keep the tasks from being done on the grounds that their monetary value doesn't fit with the social agenda. It may seem desirable to keep people from working for too little money, but keeping people who want those jobs out of work is both an attack on liberty and a mistake in economics.

If we compare life in a city to life on a deserted island, then we can better understand the repercussions of not allowing our least-skilled laborers to work for what they are worth. Take, for example, ten people shipwrecked on an island, with no expectation of a rescue anytime soon.

Let us say that one is too old to work, three are children, and the other six are capable adults. We assume that the six adults and the three children will work to build and maintain shelters, find and deliver clean water, and locate and cook food for all ten people.

Now suppose that three of the adults start businesses in which each takes care of one of the main tasks on the island. They each hire one other adult and one child to help accomplish their daily tasks. The children are probably not excited about the amount of resources allotted to them as pay, but they know that it is the best offer they have (better than surviving alone) and so they choose to continue working for meager portions.

Now, what would happen if we implemented a living wage on the island? Let's say the group votes that two of the children are not getting enough food and benefits from the work they do.

Now, the two youngest and least-skilled kids are no longer allowed to work because they are not getting paid enough. By choosing to participate in the working program on the island, the kids themselves were saying that they were better off working with the group than being by themselves, and that they can benefit from group trade. However the group decided the deal is not good enough, so they prevented the kids from working.

It seems asinine not to let people work when they are trying to survive on a deserted island, just because they do not
produce as much as others. Yet, when it comes to a city, many
people quickly assume that others should not work for less
than some guaranteed wage.

Creating a Higher Standard of Living

I propose that the standard of living is higher for the people
of a city (or deserted island) who let as many persons work as
want to, than in a community that eliminates jobs that do not
seem particularly enticing. The absence of a living wage does
not require the undue work of any one person; it just protects
the rights of those least-skilled people who want to work,
while providing services that increase everyone's standard of
living, including the workers' own.

---

*If eight dollars an hour is good, then why would we not
require twenty or even one hundred dollars an hour as a
living wage?*

Now let us look at the island two years later. There are two
possibilities. One is that two children have not worked for the
past two years because they were not considered productive
enough. They ran around the island, playing games and living
off the labor of the seven workers. They have not gained any
job skills or experience to make them more valuable citizens
on the island.

The other possibility is that the children were allowed to
work for the previous two years. Not only have they matured,
but they have also developed much-needed job skills in their
given tasks. Perhaps, by working they have created more effi
cient methods for delivering their goods and services. Perhaps
they have learned how to do their respective bosses' jobs and
are ready to take over should something happen to that per-

son. At the very least, they have contributed two years of production that has increased the standard of living for everyone on the island.

Increase Production, Not Wages

I use the island illustration to show that even basic economics demonstrates problems with mandated wages. Another argument, presented by Lew Rockwell, deals with the optimal level of wages. If eight dollars an hour is good, then why would we not require twenty or even one hundred dollars an hour as a living wage? These numbers sound absurd, but the economics that makes them unthinkable is the same economics that makes even a "low" living wage an inefficient option.

Standards of living do not increase with wages, but rather with production. Society needs people to produce at any wage, and then prices will reflect the wages being earned for a given task. Once we look at the living-wage law from the point of view of someone who loses his or her job (as opposed to someone who gets a raise), we see its ugly side.

Ultimately, a living wage in Athens (or anywhere) will actually hurt the poor rather than helping them. It will decrease production, increase counterproductive activity for the least skilled, and increase prices for the entire population. Cities like Athens should encourage work instead, by minimizing regulations on labor and allowing everyone's standard of living to increase with unadulterated production.

11

Capitalism Is the Cure for Poverty

Robert Gelinas

Robert Gelinas is an author and publisher as well as a technology executive at JPE Inc. Consulting.

The notion that capitalism is the cause of poverty, as well as social and economic injustice, is false. Though the Obama administration promotes wealth redistribution by taxing the rich and increasing entitlements for the poor, this is the opposite of what the country should be doing. People should not be led to believe that they cannot escape poverty without government help. The government needs to stay out of the way of capitalism, a natural solution to poverty that will allow businesses to thrive and the poor to lift themselves up.

"Social justice" is an oxymoron—a contradiction of terms, built on a lie.

Helen Keller opined, "Until the great mass of the people shall be filled with the sense of responsibility for each other's welfare, social justice can never be attained."

Phrases such as "social justice," "political justice," and "economic justice" have a certain egalitarian connotation—which is why they are so often used as the justification for more and more big-government programs. It's clever wordplay, for we all believe in "liberty and justice for all." But isn't *justice* about righting wrongs?

When we think of "justice being served," the image that comes to mind is a courtroom, where everyone is judged fairly. Yet when the word "justice" is appended to antecedents such as "social," it means something quite distinct from the application of jurisprudence.

"Social justice" posits a false political premise: that the economic condition of "poverty" is an inherent societal injustice perpetrated by the inequities of capitalism against an entire social strata of innocent victims, depriving them of fundamental economic entitlements and securities—a *civil rights* issue—which further contends that the only just remedy is the redistribution of wealth to achieve societal equality.

Failure is one of life's greatest teachers, and without its sting of accountability, all achievement would be meaningless.

Wealth Redistribution

As President Obama explained:

> . . . the Supreme Court never ventured into the issues of *redistribution of wealth*, and of more basic issues such as *political and economic justice* in society. [O]ne of the, I think, tragedies of the civil rights movement was, because the civil rights movement became so court focused I think there was a tendency to lose track of the political and community organizing and activities on the ground that are able to put together the actual *coalition of powers* through which you bring about *redistributive change*.

We just saw "redistributive change" when Obama's "coalition of powers," despite overwhelming public objection, shoved ObamaCare [health care reform] into law, claiming how *unfair* and *unjust* it was that millions in our country lack health care coverage. So how is this great social injustice to be remedied? Not by any effort to increase health care availability or lower costs, but by massive new entitlement legislation mandating the *redistribution of wealth*. Or, as Vice President Joe Biden noted, "You may call it redistribution of wealth. I just call it *being fair*."

Fairness Cannot Be Forced

If "fairness" is misunderstood to be the forced equality of resultant circumstances or outcomes, then life obviously isn't fair, nor could it ever be: That's why bras and jockstraps come in different sizes. Individuals will always have innate physical, intellectual, and psychological differences that affect their lots in life. Everyone's life experiences differ, from when and where one is born to how someone is raised, schooling (or not), culture and customs, achievements and failures, everything. Besides, failure is one of life's greatest teachers, and without its sting of accountability, all achievement would be meaningless.

Most of us have experienced, at least once, if not more than once, what it's like to be broke and struggling for a time.

As altruistic a notion as it might be for everyone to be able to live in plenty and for no one to be in want, it is utterly naïve to believe that the mitigation of poverty—even for equality's, fairness's, or justice's sake—could ever be achieved by means of the redistribution of wealth. It is an exercise in futility. [Former British Prime Minister and statesman] Winston Churchill noted: "For a nation to try to tax itself into prosperity is like a man standing in a bucket and trying to lift himself up by the handle." Jesus said, "The poor you will have with you always" (Mark 14:7). That's not to say that poverty is an incurable infirmity, but rather, it is the realization that poverty is but a symptom, not the underlying disease.

The Disempowerment of Dependence

We are all equally born into an initial state of poverty: entering this world naked, empty-handed, hungry, unable to feed or clothe ourselves, uneducated, physically vulnerable, and 100% dependent on the provision of others for our basic survival. From that moment, as we mature into adulthood, regardless of all the circumstantial advantages or disadvantages that fate deals us, successfully making our way forward in life is about learning to exchange complete dependence for independence, individuality, and ultimately self-sufficiency. Unfortunately, far too many people never fully achieve self-sufficiency (which can still be done even on very modest means)—or worse, they are deceived by a parasitic nanny-state into believing that self-reliance is either unnecessary or impossible. This deception is the greatest social injustice of all.

There is a vast difference between living in perpetual poverty and just being broke. Most of us have experienced, at least once, if not more than once, what it's like to be broke and struggling for a time. Being broke is a cash-flow problem. Living in chronic poverty and dependent upon government is a self-sufficiency problem. Paraphrasing the old proverb, those who are temporarily broke might only need "a fish" to assuage their hunger for a time, but those mired in poverty need to "learn to fish" so that they may eat for a lifetime.

Benjamin Franklin observed,

> I am for doing good to the poor, but I differ in opinion of the means. I think the best way of doing good to the poor, is not making them easy in poverty, but leading or driving them out of it. In my youth I travelled much, and I observed in different countries, that the more public provisions were made for the poor, the less they provided for themselves, and of course became poorer. And, on the contrary, the less was done for them, the more they did for themselves, and became richer.

Let Capitalism Eliminate Poverty

America was founded on the idea of offering its citizens the *opportunity* for self-sufficient lives and great achievement, not an *entitlement* by anyone to the fruits of others' achievements. In America we enjoy the liberty to pursue happiness, with no guarantee whatsoever of any specific outcome. Contrary to the creed of social justice, the prosperity created by capitalism doesn't cause poverty—it cures it. Conversely, the quixotic folly of social justice's wealth redistribution only perpetuates the infirmity of poverty as it diminishes the cure of prosperity.

If government really cared about lifting the maximum number of people out of poverty, it would do everything within its power to get out of capitalism's way and let its citizens exercise their liberty to achieve ever-greater prosperity.

12

Unregulated Capitalism
Exploits the Poor

Barbara Ehrenreich

Barbara Ehrenreich is an essayist, book author, and social critic.

The credit crisis is proof that unchecked capitalism ends in disaster. Wal-Mart offers an example of how today's workers don't even make enough to buy the cheap goods they produce. Low wages, together with easy credit and predatory mortgage-lending, have put the working poor at the bottom of an economic house of cards.

Somewhere in the Hamptons a high-roller is cursing his cleaning lady and shaking his fists at the lawn guys. The American poor, who are usually tactful enough to remain invisible to the multi-millionaire class, suddenly leaped onto the scene and started smashing the global financial system. Incredibly enough, this may be the first case in history in which the downtrodden manage to bring down an unfair economic system without going to the trouble of a revolution.

First they stopped paying their mortgages, a move in which they were joined by many financially stretched middle class folks, though the poor definitely led the way. All right, these were trick mortgages, many of them designed to be unaffordable within two years of signing the contract. There were "NINJA" loans, for example, awarded to people with "no income, no job or assets." Conservative columnist Niall Fergusen laments the low levels of "economic literacy" that allowed people to be exploited by sub-prime loans. Why didn't these low-income folks get lawyers to go over the fine print? And don't they have personal financial advisors anyway?

Then, in a diabolically clever move, the poor—a category which now roughly coincides with the working class—stopped shopping. Both Wal-Mart and Home Depot announced disappointing second quarter performances [in 2007], plunging the market into another Arctic-style meltdown. H. Lee Scott, CEO of the low-wage Wal-Mart empire, admitted with admirable sensitivity, that "it's no secret that many customers are running out of money at the end of the month."

Unfair Wages

I wish I could report that the current attack on capitalism represents a deliberate strategy on the part of the poor, that there have been secret meetings in break rooms and parking lots around the country, where cell leaders issued instructions like, "You, Vinny—don't make any mortgage payment this month. And Caroline, forget that back-to-school shopping, OK?" But all the evidence suggests that the current crisis is something the high-rollers brought down on themselves.

Somehow, no one bothered to figure out where the poor were going to get the money to pay for all the money they were being offered.

When, for example, the largest private employer in America, which is Wal-Mart, starts experiencing a shortage of customers, it needs to take a long, hard look in the mirror. About a century ago, Henry Ford realized that his company would only prosper if his own workers earned enough to buy Fords. Wal-Mart, on the other hand, never seemed to figure out that its cruelly low wages would eventually curtail its own growth, even at the company's famously discounted prices.

The sad truth is that people earning Wal-Mart-level wages tend to favor the fashions available at the Salvation Army. Nor do they have much use for Wal-Mart's other departments, such as Electronics, Lawn and Garden, and Pharmacy.

Unethical Lending Practices

It gets worse though. While with one hand the high-rollers, H. Lee Scott among them, squeezed the American worker's wages, the other hand was reaching out with the tempting offer of credit. In fact, easy credit became the American substitute for decent wages. Once you worked for your money, but now you were supposed to pay for it. Once you could count on earning enough to save for a home. Now you'll never earn that much, but, as the lenders were saying—heh, heh—do we have a mortgage for you!

Pay day loans, rent-to-buy furniture and exorbitant credit card interest rates for the poor were just the beginning. In its May 21st [2007] cover story on "The Poverty Business," *BusinessWeek* documented the stampede, in just the last few years, to lend money to the people who could least afford to pay the interest: Buy your dream home! Refinance your house! Take on a car loan even if your credit rating sucks! Financiamos a Todos![1] Somehow, no one bothered to figure out where the poor were going to get the money to pay for all the money they were being offered.

Personally, I prefer my revolutions to be a little more proactive. There should be marches and rallies, banners and sit-ins, possibly a nice color theme like red or orange. Certainly, there should be a vision of what you intend to replace the bad old system with—European-style social democracy, Latin American-style socialism, or how about just American capitalism with some regulation thrown in?

Global capitalism will survive the current credit crisis; already, the government has rushed in to soothe the feverish

1. Spanish for Financing for all.

markets. But in the long term, a system that depends on extracting every last cent from the poor cannot hope for a healthy prognosis. Who would have thought that foreclosures in Stockton and Cleveland would roil the markets of London and Shanghai? The poor have risen up and spoken; only it sounds less like a shout of protest than a low, strangled, cry of pain.

13

Africa Needs Trade More than Aid

William Easterly

William Easterly is Professor of Economics at New York University, and co-director of its Development Research Institute.

Western media and celebrity activists portray Africa stereotypically, mired in helpless destitution, when in fact the continent is making economic and social strides. While many African countries are still very poor, markers such as rises in gross domestic product, as well as cell phone and Internet use, should be celebrated and encouraged. Those who want to help Africa should consume more African goods and create less negative propaganda.

Just when it seemed that Western images of Africa could not get any weirder, the July 2007 special Africa issue of *Vanity Fair* was published, complete with a feature article on "Madonna's Malawi." At the same time, the memoirs of an African child soldier are on sale at your local Starbucks, and celebrity activist Bob Geldof is touring Africa yet again, followed by TV cameras, to document that "War, Famine, Plague & Death are the Four Horsemen of the Apocalypse and these days they're riding hard through the back roads of Africa."

A More Realistic Picture

It's a dark and scary picture of a helpless, backward continent that's being offered up to TV watchers and coffee drinkers. But in fact, the real Africa is quite a bit different. And the problem with all this Western stereotyping is that it manages to snatch defeat from the jaws of some current victories, fueling support for patronizing Western policies designed to rescue the allegedly helpless African people while often discouraging those policies that might actually help.

Let's begin with those rampaging Four Horsemen. Do they really explain Africa today? What percentage of the African population would you say dies in war every year? What share of male children, age 10 to 17, are child soldiers? How many Africans are afflicted by famine or died of AIDS [acquired immunodeficiency syndrome] last year or are living as refugees?

It's too soon to conclude that Africa is on a stable growth track, but why not celebrate what Africans have already achieved?

In each case, the answer is one-half of 1% of the population or less. In some cases it's much less; for example, annual war deaths have averaged 1 out of every 10,800 Africans for the last four decades. That doesn't lessen the tragedy, of course, of those who are such victims, and maybe there are things the West can do to help them. But the typical African is a long way from being a starving, AIDS-stricken refugee at the mercy of child soldiers. The reality is that many more Africans need latrines than need Western peacekeepers—but that doesn't play so well on TV.

Small Victories Lead to Progress

Further distortions of Africa emanate from former British Prime Minister Tony Blair's star-studded Africa Progress Panel (which includes the ubiquitous Geldof). The panel laments in its 2007 news release that Africa remains "far short" of its goal of making "substantial inroads into poverty reduction." But this doesn't quite square with the sub-Saharan Africa that in 2006 registered its third straight year of good GDP [Gross

Domestic Product] growth—about 6%, well above historic averages for either today's rich countries or all developing countries. Growth of living standards in the last five years is the highest in Africa's history.

The real Africa also has seen cellphone and Internet use double every year for the last seven years. Foreign private capital inflows into Africa hit $38 billion in 2006—more than foreign aid. Africans are saving a higher percentage of their incomes than Americans are (so much for the "poverty trap" of being "too poor to save" endlessly repeated in aid reports). I agree that it's too soon to conclude that Africa is on a stable growth track, but why not celebrate what Africans have already achieved?

Instead, the international development establishment is rigging the game to make Africa—which is, of course, still very poor—look even worse than it really is. It announces, for instance, that Africa is the only region that is failing to meet the Millennium Development Goals[1] (MDGs in aid-speak) set out by the United Nations. Well, it takes extraordinary growth to cut extreme poverty rates in half by 2015 (the first goal) when a near-majority of the population is poor, as is the case in Africa. (Latin America, by contrast, requires only modest growth to halve its extreme poverty rate from 10% to 5%.)

Why do aid organizations and their celebrity backers want to make African successes look like failures?

This is how Blair's panel managed to call Africa's recent growth successes a failure. But the reality is that virtually all other countries that have escaped extreme poverty did so through the kind of respectable growth that Africa is enjoy-

---

1. Eight goals—including reductions in extreme poverty, major diseases, and child mortality—set by the United Nations in 2000 to be achieved by 2015.

ing—not the kind of extraordinary growth that would have been required to meet the arbitrary Millennium Development Goals.

Progress in Education

Africa will also fail to meet the second goal of universal primary education by 2015. But this goal is also rigged against Africa, because Africa started with an unusually low percentage of children enrolled in elementary school. As economist Michael Clemens points out, most African countries have actually expanded enrollments far more rapidly over the last five decades than Western countries did during their development, but Africans still won't reach the arbitrary aid target of universal enrollment by 2015. For example, the World Bank condemned Burkina Faso in 2003 as "seriously off track" to meet the second MDG, yet the country has expanded elementary education at more than twice the rate of Western historical experience, and it is even far above the faster educational expansions of all other developing countries in recent decades.

Why do aid organizations and their celebrity backers want to make African successes look like failures? One can only speculate, but it certainly helps aid agencies get more publicity and more money if problems seem greater than they are. As for the stars—well, could Africa be saving celebrity careers more than celebrities are saving Africa?

In truth, Africans are and will be escaping poverty the same way everybody else did: through the efforts of resourceful entrepreneurs, democratic reformers and ordinary citizens at home, not through PR [public relations] extravaganzas of ill-informed outsiders.

Supporting African Trade

The real Africa needs increased trade from the West more than it needs more aid handouts. A respected Ugandan journalist, Andrew Mwenda, made this point at a recent African conference despite the fact that the world's most famous celebrity activist—Bono—was attempting to shout him down. Mwenda was suffering from too much reality for Bono's taste: "What man or nation has ever become rich by holding out a begging bowl?" asked Mwenda.

Perhaps Bono was grouchy because his celebrity-laden "Red" campaign to promote Western brands to finance begging bowls for Africa has spent $100 million on marketing and generated sales of only $18 million, according to a recent report. But the fact remains that the West shows a lot more interest in begging bowls than in, say, letting African cotton growers compete fairly in Western markets (see the recent collapse of world trade talks).

Today, as I sip my Rwandan gourmet coffee and wear my Nigerian shirt here in New York, and as European men eat fresh Ghanaian pineapple for breakfast and bring Kenyan flowers home to their wives, I wonder what it will take for Western consumers to learn even more about the products of self-sufficient, hardworking, dignified Africans. Perhaps they should spend less time consuming Africa disaster stereotypes from television and *Vanity Fair*.

14

Microfinance Can Alleviate Poverty

Daniel Howden

Daniel Howden is currently the Africa Correspondent for The Independent.

Clarice Adhiambo has gone from living in one of Africa's worst slums to having her own home in Kaputei, a new eco-town south of Nairobi. She is part of a development experiment hoping to parlay the popularity of microfinance into an even more effective anti-poverty tool. The microfinance institution, Jamii Bora, has been innovative and resourceful in bringing this idyllic town into existence, but it remains unclear whether this program can be expanded enough to help the millions of individuals currently living in poverty.

Clarice Adhiambo was looking for the usual things when she moved. Safe streets, more space, a guest room, maybe even a view of something green. More than anything she wanted a place to call her own. Her wish-list would be familiar to first-time buyers anywhere in the world. What would be less recognisable is the place from which she was moving.

Clarice left behind a 10ft by 10ft tin shack that she shared with eight others in the Nairobi slum of Soweto. Unlike the iconic South African shanty town of the same name, there is no electricity, running water or flushing toilets and no prospect of getting them. Kenya's capital offers some of the most appalling urban poverty to be found anywhere in the world. It was in places like Kibera, Mathare and Soweto that the term "flying toilet" was invented. It describes the desperate people who cannot afford to use pit latrines and have to defecate into plastic bags and hurl them on to a nearby roof.

In her new home in Kaputei, an eco-town rising from the plains south of Nairobi, she has a flushing loo [toilet] for the first time in her life and understandably she's delighted. "This place has fresh air," the 53-year-old says, almost unbelievingly.

Building on the Success of Microfinance

Clarice is part of one of 50 families who have bought into a startling experiment that it is hoped will change the nature of microfinance and banking for the poor. The practice pioneered by the Nobel laureate Muhammad Yunus, of offering tiny loans to the some of the world's bottom billion living on less than $1 a day, is flourishing. From six million borrowers worldwide in 1987, microfinance groups now lend to 150 million people. And while the rest of the banking industry has been in meltdown, microfinance has been a rare pocket of stability and growth. The sector brings together an unlikely, eclectic mix of people from frustrated charity workers to entrepreneurs, to those who have already made their fortune and come to microfinance with the evangelical zeal of the reborn.

Ed Bland falls into this last category. In his past life as a Microsoft executive he was the man who launched the X-Box. Today he is the president of Unitus, an American non-profit group in a hurry to make a big difference to global poverty and intent on using microfinance to do it. Mr. Bland explains his credo as "the ability to use common business principles to make people's lives better in a way that development has shown it can't do". In the future, he believes there will be an "opportunity for enterprising banks to focus on the bottom and not just the top". "Look what happened when we just focused on the top," he muses.

Seattle-based Unitus uses its capital, connections and corporate credibility to persuade mainstream banks to loan to, or underwrite, microfinance institutions (MFIs). It then uses its know-how to identify and support innovative microfinance outfits it believes can make a dramatic impact on alleviating poverty.

Kaputei—A New Town in Kenya

Mr. Bland rates Jamii Bora, Kenya's oldest and biggest MFI, among the most innovative organisations in the world. When Jamii Bora—Swahili for "better families"—found that micro loans and repayments could take the poorest only so far, it decided to do something new.

Kaputei's houses are powered by solar panels and its water will be processed by one of the first ecologically sound recycling plants in Africa.

"As long as you are living in the slums, you will never climb out of poverty," says Ingrid Munro, the founder of Jamii Bora. "Families of course need economic opportunities to rise out of poverty but what good are they if you are still living in hell?" The solution they came up with was to build an entirely new town, a Milton Keynes[1] of microfinance.

The result is Kaputei with its neat rows of clay-tiled roofs. From a distance, it looks like the shining town on a hill, only this one is set among Maasai grazing lands and the occasional polythene flower farm. "We are seeing something that we haven't seen anywhere else in the world," says Mr. Bland, bumping along the dirt track towards it in a mini-bus.

When Jamii Bora found that the Kenya power corporation wanted a fortune to connect the town to the grid, their atti-

---

1. A new town in Britain in 1967. Milton Keynes was part of the New Towns Movement that began in 1946 to improve living conditions for those residing in war-torn areas with damaged infrastructure.

tude was "we'll do it ourselves". So they built their own renew-able power station. When builders' merchants wanted to over-charge for breeze blocks and tiles, they built their own factories which now provide jobs as well as materials. Kaputei's houses are powered by solar panels and its water will be processed by one of the first ecologically sound recycling plants in Africa.

The question is whether Kaputei is scaleable. Even if it succeeds in getting 2,500 families to move from the slums, it is a pressure release that will be barely felt in the likes of Kib-era, with its one-million plus residents.

The Beginning of the Experiment

Relaxing in an armchair in her sitting room, Clarice gives the former Microsoft whizzkids her take on where Jamii Bora's fe-rocious can-do mentality comes from. It is an organisation she knows well, having joined at the "ground level".

Born into poverty near Lake Victoria, Clarice had a hard life. She was badly beaten by her husband and the father of three of her four children. He eventually threw her out and she drifted from friend to relative before ending up a street beggar in Nairobi.

While living rough she was raped, conceiving her only son. Clarice and her fellow beggars struck up a relationship with a kindly worker of a non-government organisation they knew as Mama Ingrid. As well as a little money, the Swede would take the time to talk to the women, Clarice remembers.

By her sixth loan, there was too much money for fish and she expanded into market stalls.

Despite this friendship, the women were deeply suspicious when Mama offered to help them learn how to save money. The women thought "she'd been sent from Sweden to come and eat our money" and hatched a plan to beat her up. Ingrid Munro persisted and persuaded a few dozen of the beggars to trust her. Clarice's face contorts with remembered shock when she recalls the day Mama told her she had saved 1,000 Kenyan shillings (£8).

A Mortgage for Clarice

There were more surprises to come as Mrs. Munro offered to lend her the same amount again to set up a business. "Don't give me a headache," was Clarice's initial response. "What is a loan? What business can I do? I don't even know how to write my name." The Great Lakes girl put her 2,000 Kenyan shillings in fish. With each loan repaid she would borrow more.

By her sixth loan, there was too much money for fish and she expanded into market stalls. By her 10th, she was borrowing £1,200 and opening a string of slum businesses. The first group of 50 beggars a decade ago has swollen to a membership of 225,000.

Clarice's latest loan is a mortgage on her home in Kaputei with monthly payments of £23. She is "overpaying" at the moment to settle the loan early.

From the window of Clarice's kitchen, the green of the grasslands is only interrupted by the black and white lines of a herd of zebra. But it is the sink tap that holds her attention. She turns it on. "So much water," she says with infectious wonder.

Organizations to Contact

The editors have compiled the following list of organizations concerned with the issues debated in this book. The descriptions are derived from materials provided by the organizations. All have publications or information available for interested readers. The list was compiled on the date of publication of the present volume; street and online addresses may change. Be aware that many organizations take several weeks or longer to respond to inquiries, so allow as much time as possible.

American Enterprise Institute for Public Policy and Research (AEI)
1150 17th St. NW, Washington, DC   20036
(202) 862-5800 • Fax: (202) 862-7177
website: www.aei.org

The American Enterprise Institute began as the American Enterprise Association in 1943 out of concern over wartime economic policies. Today, this nonprofit research organization advocates limited government, tax reduction, capitalist enterprise, and individual responsibility as the best responses to poverty. The AEI website offers an archive of op-eds, newsletters, position papers, government testimony, and longer monographs on poverty-related topics such as welfare and health insurance reform, as well as the daily online business magazine the *American.*

Brookings Institution
1775 Massachusetts Ave. NW, Washington, DC   20036
(202) 797-6000 • fax: (202) 797-6004
e-mail: communications@brookings.edu
website: www.brookings.edu

Founded in 1927, Brookings Institute is a non-partisan think tank that is often described as liberal-centrist. The Institute's experts provide research, analysis and policy recommendations in areas including economics, governance, social sciences, technology, international relations and global development. In addition to its quarterly journal, *Brookings Review*, the Institute publishes over 20 newsletters, such as "Center on Children and Families Newsletter," "Global Update," "Center on Social Dynamics and Policy Update" and "Economic Studies Bulletin."

CARE

151 Ellis St. NE, Atlanta, GA   30303
(404) 681-2552 • fax: (404) 589-2651
e-mail: info@care.org
website: www.care.org

CARE is an organization that fights global poverty with a special focus on empowering women to help their families out of poverty. The organization's goal is to work on the underlying causes of poverty and help build self-sufficiency. Its programs are divided into nine sectors that include Agriculture and Natural Resources, Health, Emergency Relief, HIV/AIDS, and Water. The website provides an archive of published articles such as "MDG Summit: The Talks Are Over It's Time for Action" and "Pakistan Floods: Two Million Children Will Miss Out on School."

Cato Institute

1000 Massachusetts Ave. NW, Washington, DC   20001
(202) 842-0200 • fax: (202) 842-3490
e-mail: cato@cato.org
website: www.cato.org

The Cato Institute is a libertarian think tank that researches and promotes public policies that increase individual liberties and reduce the role of government. The Institute offers numerous publications, including the triannual *Cato Journal*, the bimonthly newsletter *Cato Policy Report*, the quarterly magazine *Regulation*, and the blog Cato@Liberty. Numerous poverty-related studies and position papers are available on its website.

Benefits.gov

(800) 333-4636

website: www.benefits.gov

The official benefits website of the US government, benefits .gov was launched in 2002 to help increase access to information about government assistance eligibility and programs. The site has grown into a collaboration of 17 government agencies and provides information on more than 1,000 federal and state programs for poor Americans. Federal and state information is available about food stamps, educational grants, housing resources, health care and job-training programs. While the site is designed to determine eligibility for services, it is also a valuable source for discussions of welfare reform and the effectiveness of existing antipoverty programs, as well as comparisons of antipoverty initiatives in different states.

Grameen Bank

Mirpur-1, Dhaka-1216
   Bangladesh

(88 02) 9005257-69

e-mail: g_trust@grameen.com

website: www.grameen-info.org

Winner of the 2006 Nobel Peace Prize, Grameen Bank was started by Mohammed Yunus as a research project in 1976. The first and most famous example of a microcredit lending institution, Grameen Bank issues collateral-free loans averaging $100 to some of the world's poorest people in order for them to establish and run small businesses. The Bank has 8.32 million borrowers, 97% of whom are women. Grameen Foundation publishes the quarterly newsletter *Grameen Dialogue*.

Institute for Research on Poverty

University of Wisconsin-Madison, 1180 Observatory Dr.

Madison, WI   53706-1393

(608) 262-6358 • fax: (608) 265-3319

e-mail: djohnson@ssc.wisc.edu

website: www.irp.wisc.edu

The Institute for Research on Poverty is a center for interdisciplinary research into the causes and consequences of poverty and social inequality in the United States. It is one of three Area Poverty Research Centers sponsored by the US Department of Health and Human Services. The Institute's publications include the newsletter *Focus* as well as a large number of discussion papers archived on its website and available for download. Recent titles include "U.S. Health Care Reform: A Primer and an Assessment" and "Young Disadvantaged Men: Fathers, Family, Poverty and Policy."

National Center for Children in Poverty

215 W. 125th St., 3rd Fl., New York, NY   10027
(646) 284-9600 • fax: (646) 284-9623
e-mail: info@nccp.org
website: www.nccp.org

The National Center for Children in Poverty is part of the Mailman School of Public Health at Columbia University. The center conducts research and publishes information on poverty issues and how they affect children. Projects include "Improving the Odds for Young Children," "Pathways to Early School Success," and "Social Inclusion & Respect for Diversity." The Center's website provides an extensive archive of reports, briefs, and fact sheets.

Oxfam America

226 Causeway St. 5th floor, Boston, MA   02114-2206
(800) 776-9326
e-mail: info@oxfamamerica.org
website: www.oxfamamerica.org

Oxfam America is an organization committed to fighting poverty and injustice and is one of the 14 member-organizations of Oxfam International. Through campaigns like Climate Change, Aid Reform and US Gulf Coast Recovery, Oxfam America promotes human rights, working with communities and individuals to improve lives. It publishes a quarterly magazine, *OxfamExchange* as well as provides a blog, briefing papers, and a number of other informative resources through its website.

United Nations Development Programme
One United Nations Plaza, New York, NY 10017
(212) 906-6592 • fax: (212) 906-5364
e-mail: mdg.support@undp.org
website: www.undp.org

The United Nations Development Programme (UNDP) works to helps governments address issues such as democratic governance, poverty reduction, crisis prevention and recovery, energy and environment use, and HIV/AIDs. The UNDP currently coordinates global and national efforts to help reach the Millennium Development Goals (MDGs), the eight goals adopted by 189 nations in 2000, and reaffirmed at the 2010 MDG Summit. The UNDP website's Millennium Development Goals and Poverty Reduction sections explain and track in detail worldwide efforts to achieve Millennium Goal 1 (MDG 1), the commitment to cut global poverty in half by 2015.

US Census Bureau
4600 Silver Hill Rd., Washington, DC 20233
(301) 763-2422
e-mail: pop@census.gov
website: www.census.gov/hhes/www/poverty/poverty.html

The US Census is the official source of statistics on poverty in America. Website sections cover how poverty is measured, definitions of poverty-related terms, up-to-date dollar amounts used to determine poverty status, poverty causes and projections; and comparisons with poverty in foreign countries. Numerous reports and briefs available for download include the annual *Income, Poverty, and Health Insurance Coverage in the United States* as well as *The Effects of Taxes and Transfers on Income and Poverty in the United States.*

Bibliography

Books

Joel Blau — *The Dynamics of Social Welfare Policy*, Second Edition. New York: Oxford University Press, 2007

Arthur C. Brooks — *The Battle: How the Fight Between Free Enterprise and Big Government Will Shape America's Future.* Philadelphia, PA: Basic Books, 2010.

Marisa Chappell — *The War on Welfare: Family, Poverty, and Politics in Modern America.* Philadelphia, PA: Pennsylvania University Press: 2010.

Henry G. Cisneros and Lora Engdahl — *From Despair to Hope: Hope VI and the New Promise of Public Housing in America's Cities.* Washington, DC: Brookings Institution Press, 2009.

William Easterly — *The White Man's Burden: Why the West's Efforts to Aid the Rest Have Done So Much Ill and So Little Good.* New York: Oxford University Press, 2006.

John Iceland — *Poverty in America: A Handbook*, Second Edition. Berkley, CA: University of California Press, 2006.

Robert D. Lupton — *Compassion, Justice and the Christian Life: Rethinking Ministry to the Poor.* Ventura, CA: Regal Books, 2007.

Philip Martin — *Importing Poverty? Immigration and the Changing Face of Rural America.* New Haven, CT: Yale University Press, 2009.

Dambisa Moyo — *Dead Aid: Why Aid Is Not Working and How There's a Better Way for Africa.* New York: Farrar, Straus & Giroux, 2010.

Jacqueline Novogratz — *The Blue Sweater: Bridging the Gap Between Rich and Poor in an Interconnected World.* New York: Rodale Inc., 2009.

Star Parker — *Uncle Sam's Plantation: How Big Government Enslaves America's Poor and What We Can Do About It* (Revised and Updated). Nashville, TN: Tom Nelson, 2010.

Jeffrey Sacks — *The End of Poverty: Economic Possibilities for Our Time.* New York: The Penguin Press, 2005.

Amartya Sen — *The Idea of Justice.* Cambridge, MA: Belknap Press of Harvard University Press, 2009.

Paul Tough — *Whatever It Takes: Geoffrey Canada's Quest to Change Harlem and America.* New York: Houghton Mifflin, 2008.

William Voegeli — *Never Enough: America's Limitless Welfare State.* New York: Encounter Books, 2010

Periodicals

Pranab Bardhan   "Does Globalization Help or Hurt the World's Poor," *Scientific American*, March 26, 2006

Alyssa Katharine Ritz Battistoni   "The Reality of Poverty," *The Nation*, October 22, 2007.

James Chapman   "The Generation Doomed to a Life of Poverty and Crime by the Tender Age of Three," *Daily Mail*, April 15, 2008.

The Economist   "Poverty on the Op-Ed Page," September 5, 2007

Robert DeFina and Lance Hannon   "The Impact of Mass Incarceration on Poverty," *Crime and Delinquency*, February 12, 2009

Armand Emamdjomeh   "Free Money Left on the Table," *New York Times*, April 30, 2010.

Laura Freschi   "How to Help the Poor Have More Money? Well, You Could Give It to Them," The Aid Watch Blog [NYU's Development Research Institute], May 19, 2009.

Ron Haskins   "The Rise of the Bottom Fifth," *Washington Post*, May 29, 2007.

Carol Hymowitz   "Third World Entrepreneurs Thrive with Dreams, Focus and Hard Work," *Forbes*, July 6, 2010

Kay S. Hymowitz   "How Welfare Reform Worked," *City Journal*, Spring 2006.

Mark Lang   "Practical Steps to End Poverty," *Christian Science Monitor*, March 14, 2008.

Frances Moore Lappé   "A Shortage of Democracy, Not Food," *The Progressive*, July 2008.

George C. Leef   "Prevailing Wage Laws: Public Interest or Special Interest Legislation," *The Cato Journal*, Winter 2010.

Sabastian Mallaby   "The Politically Incorrect Guide to Fighting Poverty," *Atlantic Monthly*, July–August 2010.

Paul Romer   "For Richer, for Poorer," *The Prospect*, January 27, 2010.

John Stossel   "Is This Any Way to Help the Homeless?" *Capitalist Magazine*, January 8, 2007.

Michael D. Tanner   "More Welfare, More Poverty," *Charlotte Observer*, September 12, 2006.

James Traub   "Freedom from Want," *New York Times Magazine*, February 13, 2005.

David Woodward and Robert Lebonte   "Reducing Poverty Sustainably, in a Carbon-Constrained Future," *The Lancet*, July 19, 2008.

Index

A

Acs, Gregory, 24
Adhiambo, Clarice, 87–88, 90–91
Adult workers, job-training programs for, 36
AEI (American Enterprise Institute) for Public Policy and Research, 17, 92
AFDC (Aid to Families with Dependent Children), 15, 27
Africa
    education in, 85
    living standards in, 84
    need for trade, 82–86
Africa Progress Panel, 83
African Americans
    education levels of, 24
    poverty of children in, 14–15, 23
Aid to Families with Dependent Children (AFDC), 15, 27
American Enterprise Institute (AEI) for Public Policy and Research, 17, 92
Anti-poverty arsenal, conditional cash transfers in, 10–11
Area Poverty Research Centers, 95
Athens, Georgia, poverty in, 66

B

Barnes, Bill, 66
Benefits.gov, 94
Bernstein, Jared, 35
Besharov, Douglas, 17
Biden, Joe, 75

Births
    out-of-wedlock, 45–46
    teen, 45
Blair, Tony, Africa Progress Panel, 83
Bland, Ed, 88
Block grants, 27
Bloomberg, Michael, 10
Bolsa Familia (Brazil), 8
Bono, 86
Boots, Shelley Waters, 25
Both Hands Tied: Welfare Reform and the Race to the Bottom of the Low-Wage Labor Market (Collins and Mayer), 19
Brookings Institution, 92–93
Brown v. Board of Education of Topeka (1954), 28
Buffett, Warren, 31
Bureau of the Census, U.S., 96
Burkina Faso, 85
Buying power of minimum wage, 60

C

Cameron, David, 51, 53
Capital, human, 7
Capitalism
    in causing poverty, 73–77
    global, 80–81
    unregulation of, in exploiting poor, 78–81
CARE, 93
Cato Institute, 93

CCTs (conditional cash transfers)
    breaking cycle of generational priority and, 8
    critics of, 8–9
    developing countries and, 8
    politically popular initiative and, 9
    positive outcomes with, 8–9
    proliferation of, 7
    tool in anti-poverty arsenal and, 10–11
Center for Law and Social Policy, 36
Charity
    federal government's attempt at, 27
    need for, in hard times, 29
    private efforts at, 27
Charter schools, 33
Child poverty
    African American, 14–15, 23
    effect of rate on welfare reform, 14–15
    Hispanic, 23
    Left's on, 45–46
    Liberals on, 45–46
Children born outside marriage, 43
Children of immigrants, poverty in, 23
Children's Defense Fund, 13
Churchill, Winston, 75
Clemens, Michael, 85
Clinton, William Jefferson "Bill," welfare reform under, 12–14, 16–17
Coalition of powers, 74
Collins, Jane, 19
Compassion, 14
    need for, in hard times, 29

Conditional cash transfers (CCTs)
    breaking cycle of generational priority, 8
    critics of, 8–9
    developing countries and, 8
    politically popular initiative and, 9
    positive outcomes with, 8–9
    proliferation of, 7
    tool in anti-poverty arsenal and, 10–11
Conservative Party, view on marriage in United Kingdom, 50–54
Consumer Product Safety Commission (CPSC), 28
Consumer purchasing power, raising minimum wage in boosting, 59–60
Consumer spending, 57
Cottrell, Megan, 10
CPSC (Consumer Product Safety Commission), 28
Credit crisis, 78

D

Danziger, Anna, 25
Danziger, Sheldon, 39
Denmark, social policy in, 54
Dependence, disempowerment of, 76
Developing countries
    conditional cash transfers in, 7, 8
    education in, 7–8
Devereux, Steven, 8
Disempowerment of dependence, 76
Disparities, understanding, 23–24
Domestic violence, increasing rates of, 19

Dorfman, Margot, 58
Duncan, Greg J., 35–36

E

Early Head Start, 25
Earned Income Tax Credit, 40
Easterly, William, 82
Economic downturn in creating
 new poor, 18–19
Economic growth, tearing down
 barriers to, 28
Economic justice, 73
Economic literacy, 79
Economic Policy Institute, 38
Economic recovery, raising mini-
 mum wage in boosting, 59–60
Economy, low-wage jobs in, 38
Edelman, Marian Wright, 13
Edelman, Peter, 13
Edin, Kathryn, 46
Education
 Africa and, 85
 as cure for poverty, 30–41
 in developing countries, 7–8
 need to reform, 28–29
 politics and, 33–34
 resolve in improving, 31
 supply-side policy and, 38
Education premium, 35–37
Ehrenreich, Barbara, 78
Employment
 low wage, 17–18
 targeted supports for sus-
  tained, 25
Entitlement, 77
Environmental Protection Agency
 (EPA), 28

F

Fair Labor Standards Act (1938),
 56
Fairness, forcing, 75
Fathers, lifelong effects of, 43–45
Federal Trade Commission (FTC),
 28
Fergusen, Niall, 78–79
Fiszbein, Ariel, 9
*Flat Broke With Children: Women
 in the Age of Welfare Reform*
 (Hays), 19
Florez, Hugo, 9
Food stamps, 27
 increased use of, 18–19
 need for reform in, 15
Ford, Henry, 79
Franklin, Benjamin, 76
FTC (Federal Trade Commission),
 28
Full employment, 39

G

Gag rule about marriage, 47
Geldof, Bob, 82
Gelinas, Robert, 73
Generational poverty, 8
 breaking cycle of, 8
Global capitalism, 80–81
Global poverty, ending, 32–33
Gottschalk, Peter, 39
Government
 effects of welfare, 26–29
 need to tailor programs,
  21–25
 role of, 47–48
Grameen Bank, 94
Grameen Dialogue (quarterly
 newsletter), 94

Grameen Foundation, 94
Great Depression (1929–1941),
    enactment of minimum wages
    during, 56–57
Great Recession, 57
Gummer, John, 52
Gustafson, Anders, 7

H

Harden, Lillie, 12
Haskins, Ron, 17
Hays, Sharon, 19
Heritage Foundation, 42
Hispanics
    education levels of, 24
    poverty of children, 23
Home Depot, 79
Howden, Daniel, 87
Human capital, measurement of, 7

I

Institute for Research on Poverty,
    94–95
Institute of Development Studies,
    9
Inter-American Development
    Bank, 9

J

Jacoby, Jeff, 12
Jamii Bora, 89–90
Job training, 27
Johnson, Lyndon Baines, 47
    launch of War on Poverty, 43
A Just Minimum Wage: Good for
    Workers, Business and Our Future
    (Roll), 58

K

Kaputei, 87, 89–90
Keller, Helen, 73
King, Martin Luther, 21

L

Leahy, Patrick, 13
Left
    child poverty and, 45–46
    as critics of welfare reform,
        13–14
    hostility toward marriage, 47,
        48
Lending practices, unethical,
    80–81
Lerner, Jennifer, 8
Let Justice Roll Living Wage Cam-
    paign, 55
Letwin, Oliver, 51
Liberals. *See* Left
Libertarian Party, 26, 27
    alternative to failed welfare
        state, 29
Living wage
    benefits of, 66–67
    defined, 66
    effect on unemployment, 67
    mandating, 66
    for teenagers, 68–69
    for unskilled workers, 68–69
Loprest, Pamela, 24
Low-wage employment, 17–18, 24

M

Macomber, Jennifer, 25
Mama Ingrid, 90
Marriage
    gag rule about, 47
    incentives, 53

Left's hostility toward, 47, 48
in reducing poverty, 42–49
United Kingdom's Conservative Party's view of, 50–54
Mayer, Victoria, 19
MDGs (Millennium Development Goals), 7, 84, 85, 96
Medicaid, need for reform in, 15
Microfinance institutions (MFIs), 89
Millennium Development Goals (MDGs), 7, 84, 85, 96
Minimum wage, 40
in boosting economic recovery, 59–60
buying power of, 60
public opinion on, 62
raising, in boosting consumer purchasing power, 59–60
raising in helping poor, 55–65
unemployment and, 60–65
Mishel, Lawrence, 37
Moral agenda, issues of enforcing, 52–53
Morris, Dick, 13
Moynihan, Daniel Patrick, 47
Munro, Ingrid, 90–91
Mwenda, Andrew, 85–86

N

National Center for Children in Poverty, 95
National Urban League, 13
New Deal, 61
New York City, conditional cash transfers program in, 10
NINJA loans, 78
Non-Hispanic whites, poverty and, 22

O

Obama, Barack Hussein, 33, 74–75
ObamaCare, 74
Occupational licensing laws, 28
Occupational Safety and Health Administration (OSHA), 28
Ogden, Tim, 7
Oportunidades (Mexico), 8, 10
Opportunity New York City, 10
OSHA (Occupational Safety and Health Administration), 28
Out-of-wedlock pregnancies and births, 45–46
Oxfam America, 95
Oxfam International, 95

P

Paternalism, need for, 9
Perkins, Frances, 61, 62
Personal Responsibility and Work Opportunity Reconciliation Act (1996) (PRWORA), 12–13, 16–19
Political justice, 73
Politics, education and, 33–34
Pollitt, Katha, 16
Poor
economic downturn in creating new, 18–19
raising minimum wage in helping, 55–65
skill demands for working, 38–39
success of welfare reform in helping, 12–15
unregulation of capitalism in exploiting, 78–81
wage regulation effect on, 66–72
Poverty. See also Child poverty

capitalism in causing, 73–77
changing way we see, 32–33
education as cure for, 30–41
empowering women in, 19–20
generational, 8
level of rates, 39, 42
marriage in reducing, 42–49
microfinance in alleviating,
   87–91
in non-Hispanic whites, 22
real causes of, 51–52
statistics, 22–23
Pregnancies
   out-of-wedlock, 45–46
   teen, 45
Price, Hugh, 13
Production, increasing, 72
Property, education in eliminating, 30–34
PRWORA (Personal Responsibility
   and Work Opportunity Reconciliation Act) (1996), 12–13,
   16–19

R

Race to the Top, 33
Rector, Robert, 14–15, 42
Redistributive change, 74
Rhee, Michelle, 30
Roosevelt, Franklin Delano, 56–57,
   61

S

Sachs, Jeffrey, 31–32
Samuelson, Robert, 17
Schady, Norbert, 9
SCHIP (State Children's Health
   Insurance Program), 40
Scott, H. Lee, 79

Services, decrease in available,
   69–71
Simms, Margaret, 21
Single motherhood
   challenges of, 24–25
   poverty in, 22
   welfare reform and, 18
Sklar, Holly, 55
Smith, Iain Duncan, 50–51, 52
Social justice, 73, 74, 77
Social policy, need for good,
   53–54
Soft skills, 36
Standards of living
   creating higher, 71–72
   wages and, 72
State Children's Health Insurance
   Program (SCHIP), 40
Strawn, Julie, 36–37
Subsidized housing, 27
Supply-side policy, education as,
   38

T

Tax credits, 53–54
Technological change, 38
Teen pregnancy, 45
   decline in, 18
Teenagers, living wage for, 68–69
Toynbee, Polly, 50
Trade, Africa's need for, 82–86
True/Slant (blog), 10
Two-caste system, 43

U

Unconditional cash transfers
   (UCTs), 9
Underpaid workers, 59

Unemployment
    capping of benefits, 19
    living wage effect on, 67
    measurement of rates, 68
    raising minimum wages and,
        60–61
    research on raising minimum
        wage and, 62–65
Unfair wages, 79–80
United Kingdom, Conservative
    Party's view of marriage in,
    50–54
United Nations (UN)
    Development Programme, 96
    Millennium Development
        Goals (MDGs), 7
Unitus, 89
Unskilled workers, living wage for,
    68–69
Urban Institute, 21, 24

W

Wage floor, raising to lift the
    economy, 61–62
Wages
    effect of regulation on poor,
        66–72
    living, 66–69
    minimum, 40, 59–65
    standards of living and, 72
    unfair, 79–80
Wal-Mart, 78, 79–80
War on Poverty, 13, 26, 43, 47
Washington, DC, education suc-
    cess in, 32

Washington DC Public Schools,
    performance evaluations in, 34
Wealth redistribution, 74–75
Welfare
    conditional cash transfers as
        alternative to, 7
    decline in caseloads, 14
    employment for mothers on,
        17–18
    need to end, 27
    as unfair, 26–27
Welfare reform
    proposals for, 27
    single motherhood and, 18
    as stigmatized program, 19
    success of, 12–15
Women. See also Single mother-
    hood
    empowerment of, in poverty,
        19–20
    poverty in families headed by,
        22–23
Worker buying power, long-term
    fall in, 55, 57–58
Workfare, 27
Working poor, skill demands for,
    38–39

Y

Yunus, Mohammed, 94

Z

Zoning, 28